Take My Hand Walk With Me

Ramona Seath-Lübke

Printed by
Remnant Publications

Copyright©1998 by
Ramona Seath–Lübke

**Take My Hand
Walk With Me**

Cover art by Ramona Seath–Lübke

This Edition Published 1998
Printed in the United States of America

ISBN 0-9669728-0-5

All Rights Reserved

Acknowledgments

When I look back over the past several years of my life—saving moments on paper that one day might make a book, now seems incredible that it really has happened. So many living souls have touched my life with knowledge, beauty and understanding. Sometimes in the dark of night when I have laid down my cares of the day the horrible thought haunts me . . . Did I fail to mention someone or something that made this book possible? Some had just the right answers to unknown questions and others added strength to my lingering heartaches.

There were Daisy, Jan, Ann and David that gave me guidance and support on my winding journey from start to finish.

My grateful thanks goes to Papa, Diana, Calvin, Bob, Mary Helen, Theresa, Penina, Sally, Lila, Judy and Antoinette for their loyalty to me as friends and for their undying inspiration to follow through with my mission.

Very special thanks to Hugh Martin . . . composer of: "Have Yourself A Merry Little Christmas"—for all his inspiration and wonderful encouragement to keep singing for the Lord.

My sweet thanks to all those dear to my heart—family, children, special friends, and our heavenly Father. I love all of you!

The Lord is My Shepherd I Shall Not Want. . . .

These were the words that echoed over and
over again as I lay sleeping that horrible night. The
night that brought death to my beloved son. Since that
night "The Lord is my Shepherd—I shall not want"
has become my sanctuary. This book is
lovingly dedicated in memory
to my young son
Mark.

Alone

Last night the wind was blowing
The darkness grabbed me tight

Eliza step down here beside me—
and gift our minds with olden light.

The times we ran and played so hard
The times we laughed and cried

What joy when all was well—
Children, aunts and uncles galore,
in Grandma's house over the hill.

Now, we sit and think too much
of all that pleased the soul—

But yet of things that torment so—
But helped to make us grow.

The echoes now of yesteryear...
Filter through the trees

The fields and winds bear sounds of love—
From those no more to see

Tomorrow will be better dear—
For soon you'll too be free!

Ramona

Contents

1. In the Beginning 9
2. Reflections 15
3. To the City 24
4. On the Road Again 29
5. Saying Good-Bye 65
6. Awakenings 76
7. To Mother 79
8. God is Good 82
9. Thoughts/Thrills 88
10. Keep Walking 93
11. Human Compassion 98
12. I Thank You Lord 105
13. Tender Trap 107
14. Take My Hand 110

In The Beginning

Here I am back at my beginnings—in God's country. I feel like a child again. All around me speaks of peace and beauty. The gentle breeze sweeps through my tresses, sweet sounds of birds from far and near, an occasional hum of a bee, and the soft touch of the summer sun fill my soul with warmth, inspiration, and thought.

I am taken back to yesteryear as I hear echoes of my past. Why did my paths lead me so far from home? I am reminded now of how exceedingly beautiful the earth must have been as it escaped the hands of the Creator, how man, God's crowning glory, stood tall in the image of God. Man's home was under a blue heaven with delicate flowers and verdure for his feet to walk upon and rest—nothing artificial there. How pride, greed and cravings for luxury have driven us far away from our garden of Eden; how treasures of knowledge we once had have slipped away as each succeeding generation lost the yearning for graceful simplicity. Much of the beauty of yesteryear faded away as I walked where busy cities discharged contamination of every kind. Lonely faces everywhere, burdened by the cares of the day. Even though I was troubled by this way of life, I couldn't stop, not even for a little while. My flower garden became choked with weeds! Life passes us by until one day we return to beginnings, only to see in a near future a dark and lonely grave. While poised upon a rock, listening to the healing, rippling brook and observing the touch-and-go landings of the butterfly, I realize how precious it is to recapture moments of early life. These reflections can help walk us through times when darkness seems to march all around us.

I love living, and I have been richly blessed. I can't begin to relate all the wonderful things that people have done and do for me—sent by God. I am awed as I stand and watch. From strangers to friends and loved ones, including all places and walks of life. I marvel and feel the touch of God as I contemplate each blessing. Sometimes I'm so struck with emotion, wondering why all these good gifts are mine. And yet I ask: Why am I surprised? God is like that—wanting to give loving gifts to his children. Although I have passed through trials, and experienced a variety of happenings, never once did I doubt God's presence in my life. If anyone walked away—it was myself. God has a purpose for each one of us and He has promised to be faithful to complete that which He started in us.

None of us seem to understand why trials appear—right? And for the most part, we certainly do not want to confess to ourselves that perhaps we were even the cause of some of our trials. Of course, there are times when there doesn't seem to be a just motivation for trial, but somehow we seem to come through these fires with sweeter character and greater humbleness. Now we can share and feel more tenderness for our fellow man. Also we become stripped of pride and covetousness, realizing later, that much of what we desired was simply vanity. If trial, sorrow and tribulation can give us a closeness with our Heavenly Father, a deep caring for man, and a longing in our hearts to see Jesus;

In the Beginning

then is it not worth the pain we bear? There comes a time for all of us to reflect. We do not always like what we see and what we feel. However, cold reality freezes us into a self-voyage where God can do His polishing so we can shine with brilliance for His sake.

What I am about to reflect upon is painful, frightening, difficult, but also joyous. One's secret side is so much easier to handle, where exposure opens all kinds of fears. My burden to share my walk through life is so strong that somehow my fright seems secondary. I want so much for others to be encouraged and know that God can see us through "ALL THINGS".

I entered this world late March in a small Michigan village; born to a lovely and loving family. But all too soon, fate knocked at our door. Our precious, kind father met with a fatal accident. Father, an electrical engineer, managed the water works for the town and on occasion was required to work on electrical power lines. He made it known to employees that he would be on call for emergency situations should they fear going out during a storm. The inevitable happened—One evening Daddy was called out during a storm. While attempting an electrical repair, he slipped, grabbed a power line and received severe burns. He fell to the ground after his helper shook him loose from the line and pole. He departed from this world two weeks later. I am told Daddy had gloves, but had not put them on—(they were a new item at work). Father's doctor, with tears running down his cheeks, said: "He could have lived!" But Daddy knew his lungs were severely seared. He died in great pain. Daddy was loved by many, including physicians, lawyers, the police and everyday folk. He was an all around sportsman, semi-professional racer and loved trapshooting—

a sport that started in England. Daddy's parents were from England, which explains some of his desires for certain sports. All of the Seath family were born with a croquet mallet in their hand—a true love for most of us. Croquet, known as Pall Mall in England.

Without notice my mother was to be both mother and father to five children, including my twin and me—only eighteen months of age. I cannot help feeling deep love and respect for my mother. She did all those wonderful things that made for a sweet, cozy and peaceful household. Each day was designated for certain tasks, and Sabbath held special and sacred recognition. We were taught cleanliness and order—respect for our own family as well as for others. Though we were appointed learning tasks, there was time for summer and winter fun! I love the seasons—especially the power and magic of winter and will keep that thrill within me wherever I am. Mom had to beg me out of the snow and warm my feet by the oven many times.

Each week we were assigned different kitchen and household duties. My brother Jack used to pay me to do his duties, that is, until Mom caught him, and then he got double duty! Jack always thought cost effective. By paying me a lower wage he could be freed of his household duties to go out and make more money in the outside world. Mom, however, saw it differently. Obviously she had lessons for Jack to learn. Responsibility begins at home. To this day he is a shrewd business man. I have always had a tender spot in my heart for him. It seemed he was caught in the middle of things, for there was quite an age difference between the older and younger ones.

Each Friday evening Mom "acted out" the Bible lesson study. It was there I captured a sweet love for Jesus.

In the Beginning

My oldest brother, Ned, was asked by Daddy on his death bed to care for Mom and help her with us children—and that he did. Ned wanted to become a doctor or lawyer; even took pre-med subjects with high scoring, but neither came to be. Later he attended college and became a state policeman. I was so proud of him—my brother a Michigan state policeman! . . . and later a detective. As I recall "growing up memories," some of my sweetest memories were of running down the street to meet my brother, Ned, when he came home from work. Sometimes he had candy or other goodies, but most of all I just loved to see him and know that he would be home. He was very kind, full of inner strength, and good for us. He fulfilled many empty spots and had his very own unique personality. He was quite tall, handsome, and the captain of his high school football team. He was chased by all the girls! Ned was complicated, not always understood, but stirred the depth of one's soul. To him—knowledge was power.

Each Sunday I remember seeing tears on my mother's cheeks—Daddy had always taken her riding in the car. To this day, I can see Mom sitting on the sofa doing some mending or such as I tenderly watched the falling tears. I would quietly snuggle up-close beside her and try to imagine what was going on inside of her mind. Perhaps she had beautiful memories of their experiences together, for I gathered along the way just how deep Mom's love was for my father. At times such as these she must have struggled to grasp one tiny bit of encouragement. Such a loss, and strapped with five little children for whom to provide love and caring! Mother never married while we were young in fear of possible adverse influences. She had some wonderful admirers for she was very pretty and intelligent, and of course some pursuers were not so delightful! One married, rich gentleman told her she could have a new Buick parked in her driveway if "she played her cards right"—I will leave the answer she gave to your imagination. Mom had developed a great love for horses and became a good rider and maintained that love until her death.

It sounds as though everything was quite satisfactory. But we were piloted through all the phases of "growing up" developing a strong bond of love that has adhered through the years. Being one of the youngest of a family of three boys and two girls, made for highly interesting segments of joy, pain and laughter. Also, being the youngest, I got to be the observer more than the actor, yet my sis said: "You were an actor all your life".

My sister and brothers seemed to inherit all the English wit and comical qualities. Our ancestry stems from both England and Canada. As for myself, I maintained a quiet humor, but always appreciated their ability to keep others amused by creating a smile or laughter. Father had a well developed sense of humor (I am told) which obviously rubbed off on us.

2

Reflections

All of us children love to reminisce when we get together. One summer day grandpa was plowing the field and he had my brother Ned drive his caterpillar tractor. Quickly and unexpectedly Ned hit a huge rock and grandpa hollered to Ned: "Whoa, whoaa, whoaaaa!" Ned didn't hear him and hit him. Grandpa and plow went about four feet in the air—landed in a rock pile. That was the end of the plow. It should have been the end of Ned and grandpa!

Ned had some corn silk and asked my brother Jack where he could smoke it. Jack said: "You can smoke it in the outhouse!" Grandpa happened along while Ned was puffing away, saw the smoke and yelled out: "Martha, Martha (grandma), the outhouse is on fire!" Ned didn't try THAT again!

Grandpa, one day was complaining about one of the young neighbor boys. When he drove by their house, he passed with such speed that usually one of the chickens got hit and that would be the supper meal. This particular day grandpa said: "Any day that boy is going to kill himself for speeding down the roads." Later that day grandpa drove to town, and on his way he rolled his car over in a ditch. He was only traveling ten miles per hour.

We had a cousin, Jimmy, that grandpa was not particularly fond of. He brought his girlfriend to our grandparents' home to teach her to drive. Grandpa had his car parked down by some pear trees—a beautiful Pontiac. The girlfriend roared the motor on Jimmy's car, put her foot way down on the gas, let out the clutch, and took off like a jet. She got grandpa's fender. It just rolled down the driveway—took the fender clean off! Grandpa yelled out, and was flapping his hands: "Wait, Jimmy, wait! I'll move the windmill."

Mickey (my sister), Ned and Jack (my brothers), played bridge a lot together. Mickey loved to play bridge, but she did not like to lose. One night she lost most of the night. She cried and cried. She nearly went through a whole box of Kleenex. Jack said: "Why do you play bridge? If I cried like that I would give the game up." With no response she continued playing! Sometimes she would throw the whole deck of cards across the room. What a gal though! She was so loved, by all of us.

Jack was going hunting one time with his twenty-two. Grandpa said: "You'll never get nothin' with that gun boy. You can't shoot a rabbit with a twenty-two," but the rabbit took off in front of Jack. He got the rabbit, so grandpa said: "Okay Jack, I'll give you fifty cents."

One year Jack wanted to go to the fair. Grandpa gave him fifty cents. It was seven miles to town. He started out, but not one car passed by. He arrived at the fair. Everything at the fair was a nickel, the merry-go round; all the things were a nickel, except the hamburgers—they were ten cents. Jack said: "I smelled that hamburger, and man it smelled good, but I thought I could get something to eat when I got home so I didn't spend money for that. I don't remember the other things I did, but can you imagine everything just for a nickel? Those were the good ol' days."

Our sister Mickey (Maxine) made us peanut brittle when

we were kids. Oh, how we looked forward to those times. Sometimes she made us do our chores before we got peanut brittle. But she always kept her promise! She devoted much of her young years to us children—a wonderful sister in many ways! She maintained a keen sense of humor though sometimes she had nothing to be cheerful about. She radiated strength of character until a time when we watched her dodging a mouse by hurriedly climbing on a chair.

While Mom was very sharp in practical affairs, Mickey was very artful in turning things about to suit her needs. As stated by Mom: "Mickey had Daddy wrapped around her little finger." Daddy felt Mickey should not be a Cinderella, not at least until the prince found her. Of course I can't complain for I'm told Daddy carried me all around town showing me off. How I wish I could remember that—just to feel the love and caring of a father. Life has given me father-like figures, and I am so grateful. Still my being will always yearn for that empty spot in my heart for the rest of my life.

Mom also had her wonderful stories. She was an avid reader, as was her father, and added much wisdom to our lives. She read to us children all the time at home. One thing we especially loved about her—when we, the children, picked on her unjustly, she had a clever way of putting us in our place. (However, if criticism was deserved, she quickly owned up!)

Not too long ago my brother Jack and I were driving rather fast, as we were running behind time for an appointment with my twin Bob. I swerved around a curve in the road and Jack said: "That's a bad curve sis, at least it was until you straightened it out."

Jack loves to tell about one of his patrons that frequents his barber shop. Patron to Jack: "I want you to leave one sideburn longer than the other and one side of the back of my head shorter than the other side." "I can't do that" states Jack. "Why not?" says the patron. "You did it that way last time I was here."

Jack was driving home from work one evening when a man hit Jack's car with his car. The man jumped out of his car and said: "Don't call the police! Oh, please don't call the police! I'll get in touch with you." The man started to walk away. Jack said: "You don't have my telephone number and I don't have yours." Jack waited for a call from him, but the call never came. He attempted to reach him several times. Finally, Jack told the man's wife that he had to notify the police. "What will they do?" asked the wife. "They will probably put him in jail." The wife pleaded: "Please don't call the police." "Why not?" She replied: "He already is in jail today!"

One of our cousins borrowed money from Jack and wouldn't pay it back. Mickey (our sister) said: "He does have many talents." "Right" states Jack. "$150.00 worth of hidden talent."

Last summer I was approaching my niece's home on foot when I overheard them discussing people that talked about them all the time. I hollered through the window: "You can stop talking about me now." They said: "We're not finished yet—stay away a little longer."

Long ago, very long ago, on a cold winter night, Jack decided to put some "Baker's" chocolate outside on the front porch to chill so he could eat it while Mom was going through our Bible lesson studies. It was Friday night, everyone had their baths, the house was all cozy, and Jack was now singing loudly while he walked to the door and made his way to the front porch. All of a sudden we heard these horrible outbursts of sobs. We had this wonderful little bulldog named "Mitzi;"

someone had let her out on the front porch, not knowing that Jack had put his chocolate there to chill. You guessed it right. Mitzi scooted through the door licking her chops. We felt terrible for our brother, yet found our laughter uncontrollable!

Ray (friend of the family), Jimmy Shore (our cousin) and Jack were driving "haul-a-ways" out of New York. The "cops" pulled Jack over to check his papers. As they were checking his papers at the side of the road, there came a big roar. . . . It was Jimmy. He just flew around them, one wheel was in the ditch. The policeman said: "Is that one of your guys? Where is he going?" My brother said: "I don't know! But if he comes back as fast as he went he won't be gone long."

One day Mother told Ned and Jack to do the dishes. They started the dishes, but Ned took off towards school. Jack yelled: "Come back and help, Mother told you to help with the dishes." But Ned kept right on going, just a tearin' down the road. He was easy to spot—a "towhead"—very blonde in those days. Jack continued to holler at the top of his voice what Mom had said. Jack grabbed a little flat rock, and it got Ned right on the top of his head. The blood started flowing. Jack was terribly scared. He said: "Buddy, you don't have to do the dishes. I'll do them for you." Ned went on to school, with no further complaints!

Years ago, several of us cousins were on our way to Grand Rapids, Michigan. That was such a treat, for back then we rarely got to leave our small town. Our Uncle Louis bought a big sack of candy for all of us. Soon his children began to fight over who would hold the candy. Uncle Louis leaned over the back seat and said: "Stop fighting over the candy." They continued to fight anyway! So Uncle Louis reached back, took the candy, opened the window and that was the last we saw of the candy. He threw it out the window, it hit a telephone pole and it burst all over the place. For miles there was not a peep out of anyone.

All of us kids like to look back to the time when we would walk seven miles to Grandma and Grandpa's house. She baked the best bread and it would be waiting for us. Nothing has tasted like it since. The winters would get so cold, thirty below zero many times. Grandma would take flat irons, heat them on the stove; then take them upstairs and put them between our flannel sheets before we got into bed. What a sweetheart she was. We would gather around the old potbelly stove—it was really cold! We loved the times we got snowed in with the wind screaming and howling through the tiny cracks of doors and windows. We didn't have to go to school on those days of heaped up snow and long blizzards. Grandma Shore was so immaculate. Her house was very clean! She had medals all around from her dramatic speaking days as an elocutionist.

It seems as though Jack was the center of all the happenings. Perhaps he was the most funny!

It has been fun sharing all the good ol' times. How often we wish to walk back in time. Memories are so wonderful, but can also be sad.

Words were not wasted as I recall, for Mom believed time was precious and belonged to God. Still, she had a sweet disposition, interweaving sparkles of joy with discipline.

Growing up, many hours were spent on the farm. My grandfather became as my father (as well as my older brother Ned). Grandfather loved me so much. He took me for walks in the woods—there he taught me about animals, flowers and nature. He also taught me about origins of certain drugs, edible berries and how to determine the age of a tree, as well as many other things. On the farm I learned about planting, weeding and chores—but I must say they are not among my greatest of gifts! I loved to fetch the cattle with old "Shep," the collie. Grandpa tried to teach me how to milk cows until he got squirted in the eye one too many times—that too became a lost art. I can however credit my horsemanship to him. I took many falls from the horse—even gashing the side of my face with one fall—scaring my grandma half to death. After many hours of repeated instruction and falls, I graduated to solo riding without my grandfather.

Great-grandfather Shore built the Shore homestead. To this day it is cherished and loved. He also built a cabin by a lake soon after his arrival from England, where several of the family members were born—Great-grandfather Shore came from England and Grandma Shore (Fleming) came from Quebec, Canada. I will always be impressed with the charm my grandfather possessed. He was a prolific reader. Many picked his brains for information—he was known to many as another Abe Lincoln and Will Rogers ("Homespun Philosopher"). He was able to express his opinions with such ease. He loved to dream—and his fun dream was to go west. Well, he never got to go, but his sons did.

The winter blizzards and early morning trips to the barn in the heaped snow are such a thrill to look back on, though I suppose I made those early-morning journeys to the barn with some hesitation. For those who have never lived through pastoral events, do not let life pass you by without this joy. You will not have fully lived without it! For those of us who have, know the thrill and excitement of watching aunties, uncles and cousins appearing from over the hills and through the woods to Grandmother's house. Was there any better food and fun than those special gatherings?

My aunties and uncles touched my heart so deeply. Each one has played such an important role in the imprinting of my life. I love to think about how they walked through the blizzards of winter to attend school. The old country schoolhouse still stands—not too far from the Shore homestead. My twin brother also was privileged to attend the "old country schoolhouse."

Grandma Shore taught piano to all my aunts and Mother. Aunt Lucille, at the age of four (as I was told), would put her ear to the keyboard to hear sounds—she learned to play by ear early in life, but later Grandma encouraged her to play some by note also. As a child I would sit at Grandma's organ and compose music. Grandma would say: "Honey, that is beautiful!" Today, I have her to thank for my piano abilities, as well as my mom.

I am so thankful that God blessed me with so many loving loved ones. The memories alone create a sanctuary from pain and loneliness.

Today, only two aunts survive. My Aunt Pauline makes me feel as though my mother still lives. She is one of my earthly angels. My Aunt Flossie is also very precious. I just don't see her because of distance.

Grandmother taught me things that through my life I have continued to draw on for my strength and growth. My grandparents and mother were very colorful and of interesting character. Grandma was a midwife and elocutionist. The latter was during her younger days. She never lost a mother or a baby . . . quite remarkable for she spent much time at it. Most physicians, during their medical careers, lose at least one mother.

When I was eleven years of age, my childless aunt and uncle (Mother's brother) from the great west appeared on the scene, and seeing that Mom had twins, immediately proposed taking me home with them for "a while." The "a while" developed into not letting go. Gifts of material worth, attention, fun and closeness escalated into disaster. Mom was unable to give me up and it became a terrible life-long heartache for all concerned; an imprint never to be forgotten. My aunt and uncle did so many things with me—ice-skating, hiking up Mount Rainer, playing with bears (the bears that were friendly), and horseback riding. I had everything any child could dream of. I early learned to appreciate the natural world—the song of a bird, the glory of sunrise and sunset, the majestic mountaintops and the wonders of moon and stars. My uncle was another one of those father figures! But with all this, I was longing for home—my mother, brothers and sister and my grandparents. The voice of Mother coming through the telephone wires and silence in her letters spoke to my heart of her yearning for her "little girl." Soon I was standing with two broken hearts and arms about me as if never to let go—but the bus claimed me and my aunt never looked back. With more understanding of life today, I am better equipped to feel the pain of two people who had lived for children they never had—I was their answer to prayer, but even I became part of a horrible nightmare. At this moment, as I speak of this experience, I swell up inside, for what was once a great joy became a never-forgotten heartache. My auntie especially lost her warmth for my mom, and so she is to this day.

I remember this as the beginning of heartaches. Jesus was my friend and He helped me through my pain. I felt the torment within my mom, and that gave me strength to say good-bye to a fun experience and to two people who loved me so much.

3

To The City

Soon another heartache. Mother decided I should be in a Christian school, and that meant leaving home because Christian schools were not in our small town. At the age of thirteen, I set out for the city to live with my sis and her tribe. Of course that had its thrills and advantages, but as a rule it is very difficult to be removed from one who loves and cares for us whatever our faults—and this was no exception. I learned early the lonely feelings of being without my mother close by my side. The times I longed for my mother's love, deep caring, talks, walks and closeness came back to haunt me ever so much! When I was outside my mom would watch over me carefully, and while in the house she would point me toward music or reading. She talked about how one day I would be able to play the piano and not be ashamed, if I took time each day to practice. Mom would be in the kitchen making dinner when many times I would hear from a distance: "sharp your F or flat your B". I loved it when Mother would say: "We're leaving for Grandpa and Grandma's farm—it's blackberry picking time." Since I didn't have a daddy, Grandpa gave me his time. He helped pick the berries with us. Today I enjoy so much thinking about the many rides to town with Grandpa. How thrilling passing over the bridge with Grandpa dressed in a white shirt, rolled up sleeves and dark pants. He was truly a man of male stability. That old bridge stands today. Mom made all of our clothes, and my twin and I dressed alike for several years! Sometimes I refused to wear warm stockings when the weather became chilly. I thought they made me look underprivileged. Of course my mom always won those battles, but my reward was being free of runny nose and sore throat.

I retain a certain shyness, and leaving my mom and some country life to be thrown in the big city I wasn't equipped for caused me much apprehension!

Let me add here that my stay with my sister did bring me in close contact with my nephew and niece. The beautiful memories of our growing days together has given me years of comfort and inspiration. They (Monty and Dee) are profound and joyful to be around. Many times I came close to returning home to Mom. Somehow a voice within me helped me to trust God with my situation. I loved Christian schooling, but still longed for Mother.

Monty later joined me for one year of his junior high while my first husband was pursuing pre-med. He and I had a great time for I understood his mind and talents—but it seemed his teachers did not. He loved to study—but not his school books. They simply were not of interest to him at that stage of his life. Needless to say, Monty got called back home, but to this day we have a bond that neither time nor space will ever take from us.

Monty loves to tell about the time three tough kids in the neighborhood beat him up and how his auntie returned the favor to them—meaning me of course! Actually it is difficult for me to think back upon doing such a thing, although I couldn't stand for anyone to be oppressed, and especially one so dear to my heart. A similar incident occurred with my twin brother—only more frequently. One day, after school, I lay in wait for his assailant so that I could give him a taste of his own medicine. My twin had no further problems with that boy, and that was the end of my performance as a fighter!

Because my relationship with my niece and nephew was so endearing, I rarely got to leave the house without them. At the time I resisted somewhat, but today I'm thankful for all the avenues of growth created because of that, and for all the joy that now is mine.

During this adventure at my sister's, I was introduced to many new trials, learning experiences and the joys of teenage years.

I remember thinking it was wonderful to go live with my big sister, but failed to foresee the dramatic changes that would affect my life for all times. Being separated from my mother meant that I was under the jurisdiction of someone else. Mickey was wonderful in every way, but still she was my "Sis," and that never took the place of Mother. Though Mom was very structured, she could bend the rules when it was appropriate, but a sister seemed to feel a little superior, and loved to let me know that at times. Perhaps sis felt responsible to Mom for me and so tried hard to stick to the rules and not bend them.

I didn't have the freedom to go and come as at home, for I was helping with household responsibilities so I could attend church school. Sometimes I would have to stay in other homes while my sis was away. During these times I felt even more the absence of my mom. I was beginning to feel the struggle of life. Jesus was making a mark upon my life.

I loved having a brother-in-law. He was a father figure, and a good one. He taught me to play tennis well, helped with my studies, and did sweet things that helped ease the loss of a father. All too soon the military took him off to war. I not only lost a father figure, but needed to assume more responsibility, and that took away a lot of freedom. I must say, however, I grew up fast! All other situations in life found me adjusting rather quickly. Change and I were well acquainted.

I'll never forget the times I wanted to go to evangelistic meetings, but didn't have a ride. Several times the guest Evangelist would come and pick me up. I thought I was in Hollywood. To this day I marvel that someone so noted would humble himself to bother with a little girl of so little distinction. One night I got something in my eye, and he took me to his home, removed the foreign body, then took me back home. I suppose he became my first love. Although I was too young to value "TRUE LOVE." This man was M. L. Venden. What a dear soul, and devoted Christian! His two sons are also dynamic speakers. Both Louis and Morris Venden are pastors and Morris has written several books.

My sister was close to Pastor George Vandeman (who later became "It Is Written's" television pastor) and his wife, Nellie. Mickey, my sis, and Nellie were roommates in college. I loved it when they came to visit. Those experiences are so dear to my heart. As a child they helped to mold my character.

At times my other brothers would come and visit my sis and me. Together we created moments that have followed us through the years, bringing wonderful joy!

The most beautiful event of all was experiencing a personal involvement with God. I had a dream that has never left my deepest thoughts—through that dream I caught a glimpse of God's beauty and the beauty of His kingdom—my path through life was shaped. We wander, we lack faith, lose our way at times but as I sit here gathering thoughts and scenes of the past, I know Jesus has had a hold over me that has guided me every step of the way. Yes, He has a plan and He does not stop until that plan is fulfilled.

4
On The Road Again

Soon graduation ended this phase of my life. I got to return to my mom, to be under her wing until college called me one year later. What a breath of fresh air and joy to come again and "sit at her feet." I was a nurses' aide at the same hospital where she worked. There I witnessed the birth of a baby and awakened to a beautiful joy but also to the darkness of death. After a few nights of nursing as an "aide" I remember trying desperately to stay awake—even in nurses training I found it extremely difficult to keep from falling asleep on "noc duty". My superiors actually made an exception to my schedule. When I did twenty-four hour "OB call" in training I sorta' fell into a trance while I was maneuvered from delivery room to delivery room! Morning was such a relief.

During the year with mom we became focused upon my soon coming nursing career and spent the year making things together. One of my greatest joys at that time was making a quilt with my mom and grandmother. I used the quilt until it began to fall apart.

Mother opened doors for me that better prepared me for college and life thereafter. . . . I learned to bake bread and pies, but most of all I was taught how to pray and keep close to the Lord. I shall never let go of how my mom made God first and best in her life. Today I can better feel some of the pain that embraced her, but yet know the security of loving and trusting God. Early I learned, that doubting God gave Satan much power! As I set out on life's journey, I also learned—so many worlds we live in!

All too soon I was placed on a bus with simple belongings, a few treasures; then directed off to college in another state where my sister's father-in-law (W. E. Straw) was the president. It seemed most likely that I would have better direction under his "tender care." Three weeks later I boarded the bus and set out for my sister's home. Tearfully I was put back on the bus to college with my sister's words echoing in my ears. "We have faith in you and know that down deep you want to be in college." The days that followed were far beyond my comprehension, but today I fully understand how Jesus directed my life with purpose. There were so many times when joy, laughter, beauty and love flowed but as all of us know, there are days and nights of trial that separate us from the above. Those times seemed so magnified compared to the present—not that today's trials fail to pain but perhaps we are better equipped to cope.

I loved the results of character building but I struggled so desperately during my learning experiences. I was of a tender nature. I cared very much for my fellow man and in innocence never could quite understand all the pitfalls of some negative behaviors. I got exposed rather quickly to the unmerciful ways of some of the young—jealousies, and impatience, abruptness, selfishness and snobbery all of which manifested themselves in full color.

My sister's father-in-law being president immediately classified me as "VIP." Without a chance of trial I became the target of many. To make matters worse, I later dated the most eligible doctor on campus—and since I was a "proby" (first year nursing), it didn't sit well at all with those of higher rank! My bed got stripped, salted and moved. I got ignored. Yes! I grew! Trial proves if our faith is genuine. I trust I passed the test. I prayed that my kind attitude would one day change hearts. I had to be patient while my classmates sorted through who I was, hoping they would see me as part of them, not someone that had special privileges, but regarded and handled just as they were. After time that did come about and to this day it brings us much laughter with some sorrow. My classmates had tears in their eyes when they did finally make things right with me. I believe the hurt was more severe for them. Though I hurt, I don't harbor wrongs done to me. Throughout life we do things that hurt—perhaps it is not calculated. We need to have complete forgiveness or it holds all of us back from forward movement. When our hearts ache during trial we need to know that "All things work together for good."

All in all my college experience left imprints that prepared me for a walk through life without which I would have been cheated of my connected path. I also experienced a beautiful love with the medical resident which flowered my path with added learning. It caught us with much untraveled road and when wisdom is lacking, unions fall by the wayside. We chose different paths. Yes, my days at Madison College brought much wisdom, never to be forgotten.

As we look back, oh, the tears, and yet such depth and beauty! We begin to cherish every little moment of time, people and things that bring us joy and yes, pain, for there is beauty in all. The valleys and mountaintops with their majestic trees teach us of God's love. We see His handwriting in a sun-swept sky. The full moon peeking through fluffy white clouds on a bright starry night, heightens our sensation beyond all imagination. Our feet, kissed by the ocean sand, lift us to splendor up and beyond. The rain, and the snow with a beauty all its own, take us far away to wealth unknown.

People, beautiful people, lonely people—looking, searching, waiting. How grateful I am for each child, each youth, man and woman who has graced my walk—turning my eyes inside out. I have been brought to see glimpses of life that possess diamonds, and awakened to good and evil conflict.

Out of these people God sends friends and sometimes spiritual friends. My children are my spiritual friends. But God gives each of us a soul mate—the closest of spiritual friends. There is none other that grows with us as they do. We walk, see, hear and feel as one. We are led to mysterious paths that only God could create. Together we grow closer and closer to our Saviour. How beautiful it is to "walk with the spiritually minded"—one has no limits to explore. This is one of my greatest joys. God has blessed me so tenderly—I love Him so.

Time passes us quickly. We must take time to pick and smell the rose, to listen carefully and observe the scenery. Dare to walk barefoot early before the spring arrives unexpectedly—run and play just before the first snowflake falls from the sky.

It is good to care for our bodies and our minds; to gather sweetness and learn to identify it so that hardness fills not our souls. Treasure the birth and loyalty of a friend. Grow from those who touch us most and from those who do not! Be willing to change when upon awakening we see darkness and let us bring the spirit of God into our lives in place of prescribed rules. What beauty and tenderness we behold if we let light shine upon us.

Seek Ye the Lord

Seek ye the Lord while he may be found, call ye upon him while he is near:

Let the wicked forsake his way, and the unrighteous man his thoughts: and
let him return unto the Lord, and he will have mercy
upon him; and to our God, for he will
abundantly pardon.

For my thoughts are not your thoughts, neither are your ways my ways,
saith the Lord.

For as the heavens are higher than the earth, so are my ways higher than
your ways, and my thoughts than your thoughts.

For as the rain cometh down, and the snow from heaven, and returneth not
thither, but watereth the earth, and maketh it bring forth and bud,
that it may give seed to the sower, and bread to the eater:

So shall my word be that goeth forth out of my mouth: it shall not return
unto me void, but it shall accomplish that which I please, and it shall
prosper
in the thing whereto I sent it.

For ye shall go out with joy, and be led forth with peace: the mountains
and the hills shall break forth before you into singing, and all the trees of
the field shall clap their hands.

Instead of the thorn shall come up the fir tree, and instead of the brier shall
come up the myrtle tree: and it shall be to the Lord for a name, for
an everlasting sign that shall not be cut off.

Isaiah 55:6-13 KJV

Photo Gallery

Grandmother Shore

Grandparents-Martha, Sidney Shore

Grandfather Fleming-Grandmother Shore's father

Daddy-seated on the stool

Mother

Daddy holding the twins-
with his eyes upon me

Mother

Who's shy now?

With my twin

With uncle Russell, Mom, and Aunt Rena-prior to Washington trip

Uncle Sidney and uncle Russell-Washington

The "Old Bridge"

My beloved sister-Maxine

My sis and brother-in-law (Ronald Straw)

Brother Jack and his family

Brother Ned and his family

41

Pastor Ken Lee and wife Rosalie-very dear to my heart

Friends-Morris and Louis Venden...their father baptized me

Ronnie, Ron (a former husband), brother Bob and wife Dorothy

A moment of joy with a spiritual friend

My mom (left) with her brother Leo

The "Old School House"

Markie-my little angel

Goodbye-precious little darling!

43

Little Ramona Lynn

Billy and Louis

Billy rejoicing at Medical school graduation-The University of Loma Linda, College of Medicine

Ramona Lynn-young woman now

Markie with his daddy

"I'm over here, Mommy"-Markie

Daughter-Ramona Lynn with Grandparents

Neurosurgeon friend and Bill

First husband-Vincent Mitzelfelt

45

Second marriage-Bill Lübke

Debbi with her auntie Carol

Bill-by our airplane

My children-Billy, Debra and Louis LaMar

Daughter Debbi-"Look Mom, I can perform!"

With Ron and his parents

Debbi with niece-Tess Noel

Concert moments

Alaska cross country skiing with son Bill-The power and magic of winter

The niece of my youth-
Deanna-to her I will always
be known as aunt "Doe Doe"

A graduation gift to Hawaii-
from my son Billy

Rose Bowl (Michigan won)...
Michigan! My Michigan!

Our home in the hills of Pomona California

Billy-California Boy's Choir (third from right in back row)

Billy-New York City Opera (right)

Billy enjoying his lifetime hobby- "R/C"

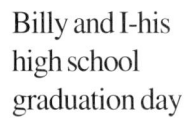

Billy and I-his high school graduation day

49

Billy's college graduation from Pacific Union College

Joyful moments with Billy, as we hear vocal and instrumental sounds of the past and present

Graduation again? Graduate of Urology-Billy (right)

Air Force duty-Billy

John, Billy, Tess, the twins (Claire and Paige)

Croquet addiction

Billy, Heidi, and children

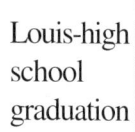

Louis-high school graduation

51

A day in the mountains-
something Louis and I
treasured

I can't believe we did that! Billy
and Louis

Wedding day-Melody and Louis

College graduation day
for Louis from Florida
State-Yea...Seminoles!

With Billy, Debbi and Louis

Third marriage-Ronald Powell

Shortly after mom died-
Louis, Debbi and Billy

Grandfather Lübke, grandmother's
Seath and Lübke

With Papa dearest
and Mother

Capping at
Madison College
(front left)

A sad moment as I felt the pains of loneliness-I loved going to the San Bernardino Mountains and Mount Baldy-so much beauty and solitude there

Seeking tranquility

Concert moments

A moment of tenderness-I happened along this scene as I was aboard a ship

Croquet seriousness

My sister, Bill and friend from Germany (architect for the rebuilding of our home)

My wonderful friends-The Heralds...From early on in my life I was touched by their beautiful gift of music (Photo taken week-end of graduation in Maine)

Graduation-Graduate of Psychology from Saint Joseph's College, Maine

A graduation gift to Hawaii-from my son Billy and more time with precious Diana

A charming portrait of my cherished Antoinette-without her, there would not have been a graduation day from Saint Joseph's College

A few days before graduation-I had just finished my last paper! I walked outside and wow! Snow in California?

With Diana-I love her so

55

The nephew of my youth-Monty (LaMont)-to him, I will always be known as aunt "Doe Doe"

A beautiful family-mother and son performed with me for recordings and on stage...dear Sherwin and Helen

With a kind, charming professor-Dr. Michael Reid from St. Joseph's College

With my most recent pianist- dear Luisa

Brother of Dee and Monty-Matthew

Mandy-so very dear to my heart-I love that little girl!

John and my dear Annie-how sweet she is! So much they toiled for my book preparation

Cousins Dale and Keith

Cousin Louis built model airplanes with me and later we both became pilots!

Aunt Pauly, Bobby, Ned, Ramona and Jack

Home of my grandmother and grandfather Shore

A very special friend-
Toni Ann (Ballerina
with New York City
Opera

Saying goodbye to
California with friend
John and Debbi

Concert in England

I love God's sheep
"I, will both search my sheep, and seek them out"—
Ezekiel 34:11 KJV

Recording studio

Saint Joseph's Student Lands Gospel Recording

Nurse, Counselor, Student, Recording Artist, Author, Mother.

These are not merely randomly selected occupations. In fact, when all these jobs are combined, they represent Ramona Lubke.

Ramona is an excellent student in the Bachelor of Science in Professional Arts program at Saint Joseph's College. Along with work and studies, she has recently recorded an album, is planning a second, and is writing a book. How does she manage?

"I don't know how"

Talking with Ramona is inspirational. Her work as a supervisor at a large nursing center is based on her love of people and desire to help them. That spills over into the musical aspect of her life.

Taught by her mother, Ramona began playing piano at age five. She grew up in a home with great "family harmony." At age 8, she was "stood on a box at school" and asked to sing.

"Angels probably helped me sing"

In school, Ramona performed solos. She was encouraged to pursue music. When she visited Maine for her External Degree residency, Ramona sang at the Motherhouse in Portland.

Finally, she went to the studio. And the result is *Looking to Jesus*. The album includes a medley of classic sacred songs as well as renditions of other popular secular songs.

Ramona was truly inspired. She explained: "While I was making the tape I felt a closeness to God that I'd never felt."

"God has been so good to me"

Offers to sing at various engagements have been plentiful. She was asked to sing at Newbold College in London, England. She was hesitant at first, but a friend told her to "quit being so humble." So Ramona went.

Ramona's life has been a combination of blessings and tribulations. Her father died when she was young. She went through a trying divorce. Her son, Mark, died when he was just a boy. Her house burned down. And yet, Ramona says "you can make a choice—learn to be happy in your sorrows."

She turned that bitterness around. Working in psychology, "to be a listener," and singing to encourage others to enjoy and appreciate their lives. "People are really turning back to God ... (He) has been so good to me."

Plans for the future

Ramona continues in her career as a nurse supervisor. She is completing her BSPA now and plans to enter Coast University in a concurrent Master/Doctoral program. She is also working on another album. Ramona has started compiling information for a book as well, hoping that anyone who reads it will be able to "walk a little easier because somebody's already been there."

"'Angels probably' helped me sing"

And she bakes her own Bread!

When asked to talk about herself, Ramona begins to tell stories about her children. Her oldest son, Bill, is a doctor. Her daughter, Debra, studied to be an airline attendant. Daughter Ramona is now studying psychology. And her youngest son, Louis Lamar, owns a business restoring cars. Her son-in-law Michael and daughter-in-law Heidi are also great inspirations in her life.

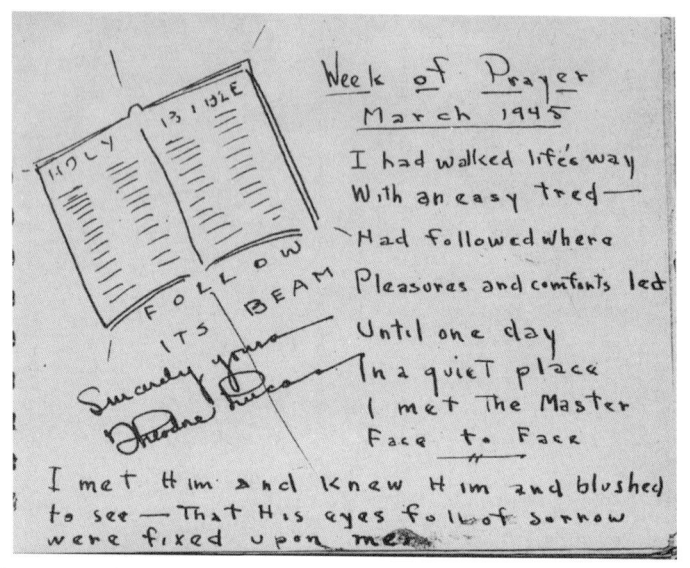

> Week of Prayer
> March 1945
>
> I had walked life's way
> With an easy tred—
> Had followed where
> Pleasures and comforts led
> Until one day
> In a quiet place
> I met The Master
> Face to Face
> I met Him and knew Him and blushed
> to see — That His eyes full of sorrow
> were fixed upon me.

A godly minister-who early in my life, touched my heart with the sweet love of Jesus...

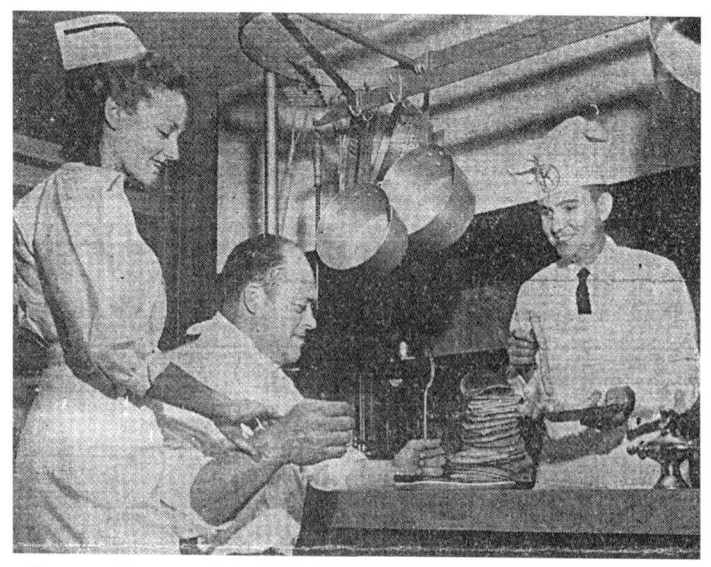

Chosen Queen of the month for Kiwanis club project...

616 734-6619   Ramona Seath-Lübke

Heavenly Melody Inc

Pager# 1-800-357-4752

Dear friends,

    After many years of intense ministry for the lord, my time has arrived! I am stepping out in faith not knowing exactly what all awaits me as I share my talents and gifts with the world. However, I'm willing to take this step because my whole being <u>longs</u> to reach out to all those who are also reaching out and searching.

    We know we have but little time in which to share in this grand and awful time. It is so exciting working for the Lord—and at the same time a little "scary" to step out.

    I had much grooming to be done in my life, and still more chipping and polishing to come, but hopefully God will gently unfold before me the areas remaining in my life that need attention. I ask your prayers and sweet thoughts as I travel from place to place—whether it be near or far. I need inspiration from each of you. And for those who have been walking with me recently and from far into my past; I thank you from the depths of my heart for your love, loyalty, faith in me, and for all the beauty and wisdom that you have shared and sprinkled upon my path. You must know that all who have so sweetly and unselfishly given to me will be with me wherever I go, knowing also that all you gave and will give will flow to all I touch. What an awesome thought—watching how we live on through each other.

    As you know, when we step out for the Lord, we need financial support as well as spiritual; anything you might desire to give will be sweetly appreciated. Never feel any amount is too small. If you can't give financially, I still need your prayers and encouragement for my strength and inspiration to continue on my journey.

    Perhaps you will desire to send a small offering every month, or you may wish to make a single offering. If writing a check, please make your check payable to: Heavenly Melody Inc. P.O. Box 172 Paris, MI 49338.

    Again I thank you for your love, inspiration and kindness. The greatest reward in living is having a part in making Jesus real. God uses each of us in different ways to make the above possible. Each way is glorious!

    As you lay this writing aside, ask Jesus to guide you regarding your part in this ministry—for it can by your ministry also. God does not need us to finish His work, but what an honor and joy that He has invited us to join Him for this precious task.

                                                In Christian love,

                                              ------------Ramona

WINNER
18th International Angel Awards
1995
Ramona

"Serenity"
for excellence in moral quality media

BORN: Michigan

STAGE NAME: Ramona

EDUCATION: Registered Nurse-Tennessee Basic Ground School-California Degree in Psychology-Maine Minor: Music-Tennessee/Maine

EXPERIENCE: Performed in Michigan-California-England-Maine-Hawaii

OBJECTIVES: Sing for the Lord to Communicate God's Love and Help Inspire Others to Think Upon Him.

HOBBIES: Music-Nature-Writing-Reading-Walking-Ice Skating-Bike Riding

Former Redlands Women Wins Angel Award

HOLLYWOOD — Ramona Seath-Lubke of Thousand Oaks, who lived in the redlands-Loma Linda area from 1978 to 1990, was a winner at the 18th International Angel Awards dinner last month at the Hollywood Roosevelt Hotel in Hollywood.

The International Angel Awards stand for excellence in moral, spiritual or social impact in all forms of media — motion pictures, television, books, albums, stage, video and radio.

Seath-Lubke's award was for her album "Serenity".

A native of Michigan, she moved to Pomona in the 1960s and earned her bachelor's degree in psychology from St. Joseph's College in Windham, Maine.

Her music ministry is called "Heavenly Melody, Inc."

"I have been singing since I was a little girl, and all my life people have commented on my voice, calling it a 'heavenly angel voice.'" she said. "As I journeyed along, I sang for my own pleasure in churches and special functions but, with the urging from listeners, for a recording. After passing through life experiences, including the loss of a young son, I went inward. It was then I decided to give that sound to the Lord."

She said she is also writing a book, hoping to encourage "those that walk in similar paths that the power of God's love and caring makes it possible for us to be happy in our sorrow."

John Grover Lewis is her producer.

The Lords Prayer

Our Father which art in heaven, Hallowed be thy name.

Thy kingdom come. Thy will be done in earth, as it is in heaven.

Give us this day our daily bread.

And forgive us our debts, as we forgive our debtors.

And lead us not into temptation, but deliver us from evil: For thine is the kingdom, and the power, and the glory, for ever. Amen.

Matthew 6:9-13
KJV

I Will lift up mine eyes unto the hills, from whence cometh my help. My help cometh from the Lord
Psalms 121:1-2
KJV

5
Saying Good-Bye

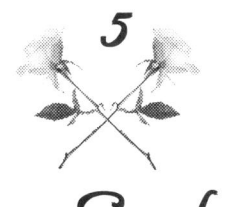

Let us travel on to events that followed college days. I married a musician who later became a physician. Out of this marriage came sorrow, but also a precious little girl was born (Ramona Lynn). There are so many factors involved in being husband and wife—background, personality, character, individual goals and willingness to understand the differences between the male and female role. Then comes the challenge to live with the differences joyfully. We did not. Divorce claimed her victims! Each one of us is guilty of hidden feelings.

Of course we fear rejection and that comes with vulnerability. It is so sad that some seem to have to experience "game playing" and false existence at times, or even a closet life—all for the sake of the above. Today the male/female role has taken on a new identity related to change of status. Our values have weakened and the home has become a place of controversy and loneliness. The world is quickly becoming too hostile. The poor youth who have no guidance or love turn to the illegitimate society where drugs and alcohol seem to be their number one companion!

After divorce and much upheaval, I remarried—also a physician. Though pools of sorrow were to become my fate, I had many days that were not silent but filled with joy. I experienced the joy and heartache of being wife and mother. Each one of us has our own touching story but no one knows the pain of the other. More children were born. There were times of early morning awakenings to catch the sunrise as it splashed its hues across the summer and winter skies. We lived up above the city, creating an unbroken view of an entire surrounding area. I cannot possibly tell you all the moments of intriguing thoughts that colored my mind as I journeyed down the path of life. Though others envied me, not one would covet what was to become my life-long cross—my Calvary. There are no words strong enough to describe the anguish in my heart.

Early one September evening, after a shared meal with special friends in their home, our precious little two and one-half year old son was crushed between two cars before our eyes. The friends were a Neurosurgeon and his family that had worked so patiently with us before my husband had accepted staff privileges as an OB/GYN Specialist at Pomona Valley Hospital, California. We had so many happy times together and this was no exception. Mark, the above son of whom I speak, was very dear to them as well as our other two children. They had asked to have Markie ride with them as we started for home. All of us were returning to our home so we could look at another house in the hills in which we lived. The house was of interest. It had a pool which was built part-inside and part-outside. All of us, including their son, our daughter and one son had started for the cars. Markie trailed behind as a young child might do—investigating as he walked. The cars were parked on a down grade—ours being in front of our friends' car. Why, I'll never know, we walked between the cars. Shortly thereafter

Saying Good-Bye

Mark came footing through. That was his last little walk—our friends' car broke from its bridle. Our little boy was caught in between the bumpers. Several attempts were made before the cars released a limp little body which fell to the ground. Stunned, I knelt down and gathered him in my arms. I shall never forget the feel of his limpness as I placed him over my shoulder. My husband took him from me as our two other children tugged at each side of me, and there my husband sat, by a fence, until our friend, the Neurosurgeon, said: "Don't you think you should take him to the emergency room?"

I leaned over the front seat as we rushed Markie to the hospital and asked: "Will he live?" There was no answer—I knew all too well the meaning of silence.

Then there were all the endless questions while he lay dying. Why couldn't I be with my little boy. No one wanted to let me by his side. In desperation I made it through the wall of emergency room staff only to lean over my little darling as he was taking his last little breath—turning from white to blue. "It can't be, this just can't be!"

Slowly but steadily I moved toward the hospital chapel—The moments that followed I shall carry with me until my death releases me from them.

I set out with this child for an evening of joy and now I was returning home without him. After walking through the door of our home with his little blanket in my hands, I stood there in the kitchen by my desk, for many long minutes—paralyzed. Perhaps to this day that is where I am still. I later picked up the phone to call the morgue. I asked them to put something over my child that he would not be cold—What a horrible, horrible moment!

Later minutes became as hours—as I lay with my head

upon my pillow, over and over I heard the words: "The Lord is my Shepherd, I shall not want." Then the sun began to send its warmth through our bedroom window. I heard gentle breezes and songs of birds that were strange to me—mysterious sounds—sounds that always echo in my memory.

The dreaded trip to the funeral home—standing in dismay as my child's clothing was tenderly placed in my hands. Too painful to even think about—even now!

Phone calls . . . flowers . . . people everywhere. . . . My life became an exhibition. Soon the terrible finale was embracing us . . . one last rose, one last kiss upon a delicate lifeless little cheek . . . and good-bye forever.

Two mornings after—oh how desolate! This was the first school day of our other son Billy. I can still see myself standing in line with a little boy with a finger in my jean belt loop. I tried to comprehend his thoughts. Such a dreadful happening for such a young life to view. I seemed to see people all around me viewing life as "just another day." I wanted so much to lash out. However, I came to my senses long enough to forgive the crowd. They didn't know my loss or pain. My heart ached so badly for Billy and for our dear little daughter Debbi. I cannot possibly convey to you the agony nor the horror of that moment.

The days passed slowly and faded into blackest darkness. I could not ignore the degree of hurt and pain for all that came to pay their respects. I felt such a sense of responsibility—I dug to the depths and pleaded for greater light. People came from near and far. Some were strangers.

Now I was alone, and wanted to be alone. There were no magic words or events to calm my soul. I needed to search for new meaning. I captured much as I went on my journey and God's words were my guide. Psalms 32: 8-10 was very helpful. "I will instruct thee and teach thee in the way which thou shalt go: I will guide thee with mine eye. Be ye not as the horse, or as the mule, which have no understanding: whose mouth must be held in with bit and bridle, lest they come near unto thee. Many sorrows shall be to the wicked: but he that trusteth in the Lord, mercy shall compass him about."

Trying to be wife, mother and friend to man now took courage I never knew I possessed. There were all the questions to answer about death to the children—especially at night when the darkness closed in on us. Questions were asked that tore my heart. I knew I must answer with strength and wisdom. I also knew the danger if I over or under reacted. If I expressed too much sorrow the children would feel they were not important, and if too little sorrow was exercised then they would fear they would not be missed should they be taken away.

There is also the pain of guilt—wondering if my life was more faultless, would this have happened? I do know God had chipping and polishing to do, to refine my character. How sweetly humbled we become after such tragedy. At least, with me this took place.

The hours of aloneness never leave my heart. I have tried to be happy in my sorrow. I want so much to be strength for those who travel the same road. It is incredible how after disappointments, passing through sorrow after sorrow and experiencing disruption after disruption that one can continue walking. To God be the glory!

I am so thankful for a Christian home and a Christian mother. The beauty and joy of that early setting has pulled me through trial after trial.

For all who have loved, treasured and lost, I need not explain too deeply. Many moons came and went finding me lifeless. Yet, somewhere in my darkest corners, a voice urged me on. There were other precious lives that hinged on my healing. That realization kept me walking and reaching out to those who were reaching out to me. I had a good husband and other children that were so cherished. To this day they bring indescribable joy and inspiration. God has always blessed me with the dearest of family, children and friends. I have made new friends since my tragedy, but some of those have become vital to me. They are gifted to be able to look inside my soul and view my heart from early beginnings. They know who I am and love to walk with me. I am so blessed. I thank God every day of my life for all my trials and joys. Without them our growth would lack beauty, luster and distinction. We gather strength and character to decorate our path of life, and, somehow in time all will be made plain. . .

After such a loss one begins to seek any new interest, always hoping the past will just die. Airplanes caught our fancy and we learned to fly. The music center heightened our sensations. Our son, Billy, eventually joined with the California Boys' Choir and became a seasonal regular with the "New York City Opera." Out of this event I became friends with a New York City Opera ballerina—Antoinette. To this day we have a bonded relationship. She has brought lasting joy, beauty, fun, encouragement and motivation to my world.

Flying places and seeking new territory and playing tennis became great "forgetters." On and on—never successful in unloading the horrific anguish. One becomes so changed that soon relationships are altered too. Very sad, but so real.

A son was born out of this tragedy. With humor he expresses: "I would not have been." Although, my mind and soul knows differently. With his (Louis LaMar) birth came some serenity for all of us. Time heals, but time never removes the ragged scars. Heaven is our only hope, where we can watch our son grow up. I am so thankful for the children I have. They have exposed me to places I had never been or would ever be without them. I feel a very spiritual connection with each child. And now I'm blessed with their mates and children who have graced my life with learning, inspiration and love.

Three years down the road our house burned to the ground. I came close to losing my life. My son Louis (two and one-half) repeatedly came to the back door calling: "Mummy, Mummy, there is smoke out here." Finally I heard the helicopter repeat similar words. Our house survived the first fire, but the second fire was not so kind. We lived up from the Los Angeles County fairgrounds. Two children at fair time were setting fire to paper plates which were caught by the wind and carried up into our hills of residence. Some young motorcyclists then thought it would be fun to light matches in our hills. That time our house was destroyed by a ball of fire that the wind gathered from across the canyon. Moments before, I heard the door bell ring, but no one was there—had I not gone to answer the door I would not have seen the momentum of fire! Someone pulled me in a car, and we went down the hill in flames. Flames all around us. We rebuilt, but somehow shortly thereafter my husband

and I just seemed to grow apart. Unaware, two people got so caught up in sorrow and the struggle to make all things beautiful again that one day our door closed behind us. The key gets lost. Another marriage ended.

All too soon another man appeared at my door. A word of wisdom—let your door stay closed for a season so you can see if something valuable is going to be lost and something new will bring deeper trauma. I married again. Oh, how dark the hours that followed—trying to adjust to breakup and a new marriage. One can never be released from all the hurt, pain and disturbances that follow a break-up. Many become trapped within the walls of others' behavior, which shed confusion, sorrow, bewilderment and hours and years of disappointment.

Some disappointments are short-lived; others affect us for life. One day I returned from work (RN supervisor at a nursing center), the house seemed deathly quiet. I called out to my young son that was gifted to us after our loss of Mark, but there was no answer. After much searching and phone calling, I was informed that he was picked up by his Father and the new step-mother. He never returned to live with me until his last year of high school. Louis was such a joy. His brother Billy had left for pre-med at Pacific Union College and my new husband was in Dental school. This created time for Louis and me to do things together. We loved to hike in the mountains, take pictures and ride bikes when we were alone. Our times together will always be cherished and I will leave it at that to spare the innocent.

We don't always understand why these heartaches knock at our door. The best I can say is that heaven will give me the answer, for the days that followed gave me a new heartache that to this day brings deep sorrow too painful to forget. I never did lose faith in God—I have always trusted Him with all my affairs, but I have a very tender heart and love deeply. Together they create anguish when life sends her arrows. It is so painful for children when the home is shattered. They have love for both mother and father, and it seems they get caught in the cross-fire. If only we could save innocent children from these heartaches. Parents should allow children to love and honor both! Many a tear has fallen because of my children's hurt and emotional pain. The witness to a broken child has to be one of the most heartbreaking crosses for a mother to carry through life. Children miss their mother terribly while they are young (even later), but also get so torn being absent from their father. Oh, if only we could do it all over and take away their memory of agony!

I have so many traumatic moments—and yes, I brought some on myself. Too late—too smart.

I had to be without my first daughter from my first marriage for many years. I try to think back on how I can fix it now. That is not possible! However, I can be loving and viable today in her life. Parents, I know many of you will weep when you read these words, they will be your words. Take heart and know that you are not alone. God does love us. It is not how many times we fall, but that we get up and climb a little higher after we fall.

By now, I ask myself—and you will ask "how does one not give up on life?" Our hurts and pains can be so difficult to quiet. "How can I keep going?"

First, I had to reach out to God. It is His mercies and saving grace that pushed me forward. I knew He longed to be close to me, and that He had never failed me. He was leading me all the way. I had to, and wanted to place importance on loving others. All I had to do was look upon the faces of my children, view their eyes to know how much my life depended on their existence. Many people leaned on my strength. All this urged me on. My tenderness gave me strength.

Previous trials and knowledge that God was always with me prepared me for new trials. They gave me strength and faith to take another step—each stepping stone of my path has its own unique story. God laid the bricks cautiously—and when I was too weak to hang on God wouldn't let go.

I love being by the ocean. There I commune with myself and with God. So many times, through many hurts I found myself at the seashore crying a river, wondering sometimes if I could lift my foot to another place in time.

I too love the night skies—celestial experiences seem to lift me from internal agony—their breathtaking beauty reminds me of our majestic God, how loving He is, and that He is <u>always</u> the same. . . . There is nothing more beautiful than to look up and all around as stars and galaxies reveal the wonders of someone greater than you or I. What splendor to behold! And to think we are children of that great and awesome God!

In Michigan I love to quietly sneak away to the lake, hop into the rowboat and row until land is no more. The sky, sounds of the sea gull take me far away—where I can feel my heart and leave the world behind.

Many times as I lay sleeping, I hear the distant whistle of the train. . . . I love that sound. It carries me away to where I am all alone with thoughts and playback of fun and laughter. Yet, all too soon comes sadness to haunt me. But something deep inside my soul releases a flow of peace—Once again my God is near. Music, my life—always a challenge. From my earliest memories I turned to the piano and song. Mother longed for me to come home from school or from college so I could play the piano and sing for her. Her favorite: "Abide With Me" and "Melody in F." Each summer I arrived from California, where I lived for many years, after college days, Mom would have the first Friday evening put away just for us to share music together. I have her to thank for encouraging this God given talent. Music—always stills my soul. It is my path to freedom. I am enthralled to hear world-class performers. I especially love hearing performances at Interlochen. What a thrill to witness as the World Youth Symphony Orchestra tunes for performance—I love when the concertmaster enters. Then the conductor approaches as everyone rises and applauds. Dreams are born and nurtured at Interlochen with development in every aspect of life—it shows in their charm and performances. These young artists with their spectacular musicianship send thrills never to be equaled.

Other thrills at Interlochen are when outstanding artists come to perform. I especially love The Lettermen, whom I have met personally—magnificent performers and people. They prove that love ballads have an attraction without boundaries and stand the test of time.

In writing, there are some heartaches one keeps to oneself—it would be too hurtful for some to be exposed. But none-the-less within the secret palaces of the mind there they lie.

I can see how God has gone before me, He has been preparing me for my earthly mission.

6
Awakenings

Yes, I suffered great things, as did my children and those that loved me. Oh, if only foresight were like hindsight. God has taught me much through all these trials. Perhaps I could have learned with less pain had I been listening and following previous knowledge acquired through the years. One does not always seem to do this, does one?

I do want to be all that God wants me to be and be where He wants me to be. I am free now. My life belongs to God and soon I hope to use my talents, especially my voice for His glory.

Through my last marriage I met a beautiful man. A gift from God. He became my "Pa-Pa." He gleaned the hidden beauty and laughter that lay deep in my soul. Many fields of wisdom took our hands and together splendor sprinkled life-long joy and beauty upon us. I became his "sweet child." He is so talented, so full of life. A wonderful witness to man. He is embraced by the sunshine he creates.

I had to experience much stress but God is keeping careful watch over me. During these struggles we gather experience, not only for ourselves but for all others who might take the same walk.

We need to invite Jesus into our lives—let Him know that we long to see Him as He is and that we want to be His servants. By serving man we are serving Him. Man is His priceless creation . . . we are so dear to Him. God can orchestrate a lovely path for us . . . we just need to tell Him that is our wistful desire.

Color, race, age, looks, mental status are never barriers with God. He can increase our minds and our talents. With *Him* all things are possible. Once we give ourselves completely to Him there is no limitation to growth, awareness, beauty or talent. He will supply all needs!

Perhaps many will be placed in the desert, as Moses, and will be subjected to handicaps. However, these times and experiences are preparation for all that God has charted out for "His chosen few."

I can't begin to tell you all that has been revealed to me, especially in the last two years, but this I can disclose—that God has become more tangible. I always seemed to do everything "their way." Speaking of upbringing, religion, et cetera, there are times we do need to do things "our way"—which hopefully is God's way. So much of my life was caught up in titles and prescribed rules that I had to struggle in my own little innocent way to see Jesus the way He really is. I'm sure my mentors did not see it that way, for all were good Christian people. Sometimes we fail to search on our own with God as our guide. All need to turn to the word of God only, for a time, that we know precisely what God has spoken to us. It is a wonderful experience. God's wisdom thrilled my soul—made me much more aware of the truth and beauty of His kingdom. God is God and He does have rules—rules to give us a better way to live. His rules however, need to fall into place because we see and feel His gentle and tender spirit. We then will long to obey and do His will. "If you love me, keep my commandments."

Jesus does love us. Perhaps we have done terrible and

ugly things but what joy in heaven when we as sinners fall at Jesus' feet because we love Him and want to be His child again! And when we combine our frail attempts with God's divine wisdom and understanding we shall shine through to others; remembering always that Satan may strengthen evil but Jesus strengthens good.

Before my last divorce took place, I felt the incentive to return to college for a degree in psychology. I did just that—with much resistance from my spouse. I so much wanted his blessing and support. It was important to me that those close to my heart be part of my voyage. I did not want to leave anyone in my ship with feelings of aloneness or disappointment. So many times we are faced with which direction on the compass to pursue. In our struggle the magnetic needle swings wildly about but light does break forth. Once again God cannot be stopped. As I recall these moments of decision and my final choice, it becomes very clear to me that God had hold of me tightly. I now know how I withstood the emotional pain that encompassed my whole being. We do have gifted power during forcible confinement. God knows our every desire and how to get us there.

My hall of memories will always hold dear all the beauty, joy and inspiration I inherited from my college professors, sisters and other students at dear St. Joseph College in Maine. They were of such humble nature. They spoke of how they valued the lessons I taught them and the inspiration I scattered. Little do we know what God brings forth from His children for we do not see good that comes from our simple little walk. How thrilling and inspiring when teacher and student receive the same beauty from each other. It flows into rivers of gentle swell that become a stage for all who stand by the seashore of repose.

7
To Mother

As I studied with great energy I had the love and inspiration from my children and my mother. What a guiding force they were. My son Billy was now nearby attending medical school.

The summer was fast approaching and I had packed my bags early to visit my mom in Michigan. I always looked forward so much to spending part of the summers with her and in Michigan where I grew up. God seemed so close in the rural setting—I could see all the wondrous things that He had designed for me. The change of rhythms that arrive with the change of seasons thrill my soul. The nights bring forth full moon with magnificent brilliance, and billions of twinkling stars like gleaming jewels that shine from sky to man. There I become so mindful of eyes to see, ears to hear, the ability to smell and move about. The beauty of the forest and the little creatures are all symbols of the Master's hand. It is so awesome all that God has given to us for our pleasure.

Early one morning the phone rang . . . on the other end a soft voice spoke: "Your Mother just died." Again the sting of death brought its intense pain. "Why did she have to leave before I got to spend some time with her." That will never be answered, for only God knows the answer. I was all packed and ready to see her in about three weeks—that was a tough one for me. I was nobody's little girl anymore. My son Billy happened to be with me. He was just getting ready to leave for school. God was good to have had him there for such a time as this.

Quickly my thoughts took me back, far into my past. I found myself searching for events that were of my mother. I knew they could only be memories now—never relived. It is such a solemn terrifying moment to become aware of the thought . . . no more making of memories. The primal pain of loss came with the loss of Markie, but somehow each has its horrible bite. She was my refreshing stream—loving me, inspiring me and giving me hope when others walked their own paths. She was always there. She, and she alone, knew me from the moment I took my first breath. She watched over me every day of my life—whether I was near or far. She called out to me when I wandered too far and too long away from home.

How strong she was—always confident even when oppositions were hitting her head-on. She had such a splendid sense of humor. One of her favorite stories she loved best was about me. Each Sabbath we were taken to "Sabbath School" and Church. My twin brother was always so proper and honest that sometimes I just couldn't tolerate his perfection. I decided this one Sabbath, at the age of five, to keep my money I had for the Lord and spend it later for ice cream or such. As my twin and I were walking home—trailing behind our mom and her dearest friend (a bible worker), I paused at a drinking fountain. As I leaned over to take a drink of water, my coins fell to the ground. At that my twin turned to me and said: "You should never steal—and from the Lord?"

I lagged way behind my brother as we continued on our way home. He had lost distance from Mother, but now he was boldly and swiftly homeward bound. I shivered in my little shoes knowing all too well my doom. As I neared the front steps of our porch, there was no doubt my mom had the news. Bravely, but shaking inside I said: "If'n, if'n you spank me I will say 'DAMN.'" Well, of course I got my punishment. Some years down the road I was told that the bible worker was behind my mom straining herself to keep from laughter.

My twin, Bobby, was however, and is, one of my greatest friends . . . a guide to the real world, always there for me—teaching me in tenderness that my character would become refined into a graceful, loving, kind and beautiful creature.

8
God Is Good

As I gathered all the roses and struggled through the rocks and thistles, God still had great things to come. At the close of college a special teacher, Dr. Michael Reid, adorned my life with an irreversible array of components that opened my window to everlasting joy and thought. I am so thankful for *all* the ways in which God presents His magnificent character and beautiful kingdom to me.

And, after all the above, graduation weekend God graced my life with a man who was to become one of the most awakening features in my earthly walk. A man who leaves nothing untouched—one who walks with God and helps to make Him more visible. Out of this, God enhanced His gift by gently unfolding a spiritual love between us that I once only knew in silence. Oh, the beauty, joy, love, inspiration, wisdom and knowledge of man yet to be explored via such spiritual connections. "We became as two secret gardens—two mysterious locked gardens...that had each other's key." Through this rare accessibility we thrive. Out of that, chipping and polishing came. One never experiences such depths without trial, hurt and agony. We soon learn the value of lasting friendship and love, and how to survive the attacks to continue on, even after interludes of <u>long</u> separations.

Challenges are ever <u>before</u> <u>us</u>, hoping that each one will give us greater strength, courage and wisdom. What a priceless gift—a spiritual love! Once given—it is never recalled.

How my life has been graced and doors in my palace shaken loose. The storehouse is open. God has a plan. We may walk through winds, fire and rain; but we never walk alone.

Many hours are thrust upon us where no friend is in sight. Sometimes only a lonely little leaf floats by our window. We cannot see, we cannot feel—we beg for God to take hold of us. Will we ever see the beginnings of a rising sun? Or will the night continue to embrace us with the darkness?

During our dry spells God's grace can be revealed. By gracious giving and gracious receiving, God's love is augmented. Sometimes hours are so dark, so far removed from reality, that one barely sees the authentic. As I write I experience such pain. I'm trying to adjust to changing circumstances. Beauty surrounds me everywhere, but I have been separated from life long friends, children and places of joy. I struggle with all I have within me until every tear is expressed from my eyes. I long for the beating wave against the rock—a familiar path to walk and the feel of the hand of a friend. Yet, a still small voice says, "Not yet dear child, not yet!"

I feel not just my anguish but the anguish of those who suffer close to me—for the agony of the world. For all that have had and have not. For those who have loved and lost. I cry out—and no one is there, not anyone. Tonight I especially mourn the death of "Princess Diana"—so warm, compassionate with internal and external beauty and grace. From fairy tale to tragedy! She, a very warm and loving mother— always trying to give her sons as normal a life as possible— How deeply pained and shocked as I think of what a loss and for the horrible sorrow her sons have to endure. I will always be touched by her warmth, love and compassion. She dared to show her emotions to make the world a better place and bring her sons to a valley of peace and blessedness.

I'm reminded of so many events and passing people of my life, all that have become priceless. Out of such I walk. The places of employment (Pomona Valley Convalescent Center, California, Loma Linda University, California, Loma Linda Academy, California, Maywood Acres, California, Charter Hospital, California and Altercare, Michigan). So many of my peers and employers gave so much to add to the character and joy of my existence. Without them I would be left desolate and without mark. I'm ever grateful for their trust and belief in me, and yes, for their everlasting love and inspiration.

My dearest friends and very very special inspirations in my life: The Vickers (my second family), Diana, Antoinette, Martha—dearest Martha—her last words to me before her untimely death: I was moved to song while on my walk early this morning—viewing the heavenly and majesty of Gods handiwork! I will miss her so—, Marilyn, Merrilyn, Mary Helen, Penina, Theresa, Marion, Debbie, Carol, Benita, Helen, Pat, Patricia, Dorothy, Pebbles, Donna, Jill, Pastor Alexander Snyman, and son Royce, Pastor Hodge, Calvin, Deanna—affectionately AKA "Danana," The Heralds and John . . . stood and stand by me with great strength and loyalty. Because of them my burden is lighter. All my brothers and sister, nieces and nephews, aunties, uncles, and cousins brought me eternity's of joy, laughter and love. Many strangers and short acquaintances have had tremendous impact on my life—wherever they are they have my deepest appreciation for helping to decorate my life. I want to thank all, too numerous to mention for all the love, inspiration and loyalty you bring to my life. God bless each of you!

Diana, my beloved friend since early years—we walk together through storm and sunshine. She is always there—when I'm afraid of the dark, I can feel her prayers and love. Her patience and goodness never weakens. I'm always concerned when she showers me with gifts and time. Her answer is always the same: "I never worry about how much I give away, God always gives it back." I am so blessed to have her in my life.

Antoinette, my dearest Antoinette—one of my earthly angels. She always has words to lift me up, and to make me laugh. She has inspired me beyond all measure to be about my "Father's business." Her words: "I wish I had your gifts girl." Yet her talents have no end.

All my friends and loved ones are wonderful listeners, and have blessed me with their wisdom and deep love—without them I would have fallen by the wayside. So many times when my way became dark and all seemed lost, they were there. I shall never forget all their devotion and steadfastness.

Rosalie Haffner Lee, a great blessing to my life, especially in my early years. She listened so intently and sweetly as I walked with her through the death of my child and so many other hurts. She loves her God so much. It radiates to all who seek her path. Her husband, Pastor Lee, also was a dear—preaching God's love so sweetly. He helped to make God real, as I took his words to heart, I longed for Jesus' return.

Marjorie Ziprick, another mentor in my music world. A lovely, charming lady and sensational musician. Everyone received her piano playing with enthusiasm. Marjorie always encourages me and introduces new light each time we talk or see each other. A very dear soul to me.

My children all have their own miraculous way of lifting me up! Ramona Lynn with her sweetness, love and loyalty; Debra with her eternal exuberant personality, and gifts of love and devotion; Billy with his sparkling sense of humor, tenderness and love; and Louis LaMar with his inspirational insight, love and closeness keep me motivated even when I feel lost.

All my children have spoken or written words to me that reach beyond this world. There is no greater joy for a mother than to hear or receive words from her children that stir the soul. My life has gathered strength, joy, love, beauty and inspiration because of their never ending devotion. I grew with wisdom from God as I placed within my soul their gifts of strength and beauty.

I would like to share with you a few words from each child: From Ramona Lynn—"you always understood me through all times, and knew how to make me laugh—I love you so much!" Debra mailed these words to me—"We have a very special relationship—it came through learning, sharing and growing. I thought at times you were too strict or old-fashioned and didn't understand, but later I realized you understood all along. Because of all the ways you cared and care I know I'm a better person—better prepared for life, it's joys and sorrows. You are my best friend. I Love You Mommy." Debbi always calls me "Mommy." Billy wrote the following words on the back of his high school photo—he was the first child to go away for college—"Sorry it took me so long to sign this picture. Mom you've been just the perfect mother all these years. But just 'cause I'm a few hundred miles away doesn't mean I won't think about you and still love you. I hope I can live as good-natured as you have lived all your life. I really mean that. I'll always be thankful for the bringing up you've given me. Well what else is there to say other than '<u>MOM, YOU'RE TERRIFIC!!</u>' Love always, Bill." Louis LaMar put the following words on the back of a school photo at age 13—Thank you for being so kind and understanding with me all these years. Sometimes I take for granted what a great mom I have. I hope in the years to come we are able to share our Christian experience together. I'm glad to have the greatest mom in the whole world. My love for you will last forever. Love, Louis." God has truly blessed me. My trials have been so intense at times, but God gave me loving children to help walk me through my storms along with the endearing friends.

9

Thoughts/Thrills

During eternal darkness we are forced to reach out. I have to reach out for God has placed a gift of singing upon me. It is my greatest yearning. Yearning to put forth my hand to those who long for God's love.

As stated, I was born in the winter, winter still lives within at times with the ever longing for Spring! While passing through deserts I pray that God will make me aware to man—that he not live alone. Let us watch carefully that one does not close his day full of desire to have shared a special joy or a deep pain with his fellow man because of self seeking. Man's tears may soil our raiment until we are drenched and then we drown. All need reserved private times, but use caution that over-indulgence take us not from a hand reaching out.

Since a very young girl I have been singing—but much for my own pleasure until people began to speak of my voice as a "heavenly angel voice." With much urging from listeners for a recording and passing through life experiences, including the loss of my son, which turned me inward, I accepted the call. God sent to me a producer at that same time who encouraged me to share my gifts with the world. God's blessings were upon us and together our music was "made in heaven."

When I was very very young, we (the cousins) used to have talent programs in our grandparents' front yard. I remember singing: "Somewhere Over The Rainbow." My twin said: "That is beautiful—you really can sing." What a way to launch my music career. Forget the statement: "A prophet hath no honor in his own country!" Shortly thereafter, if I remember correctly, I was stood on a stool in the high school auditorium and did a solo for an upper classmen function.

This last year I was the winner of an International Angel Award for my album: "Serenity." The Angel Awards stand for excellence in moral, spiritual or social impact in all the media—motion pictures, television, books, albums, stage, video and radio. I also now have a ministry—"Heavenly Melody Inc." It is my desire to continue on for the Lord . . . to keep singing for Him and of Him. I want more than anything in this life to communicate God's love and help inspire others to think upon Him.

I love music, nature, writing, reading, walking, ice-skating and bike riding. I have performed in Michigan, California, England, Maine and Hawaii, and now hope to travel to more far away places and also to places near my home. England was awesome! While I was there, my dear friend Penina had some free days from college and together we made beautiful memories that will always touch my heart. We both are very awed with English royalty!

Hawaii is indescribable—IOA Valley on Maui has captured my soul for life . . . it was preciously shared with my dearest friend Diana, who lives on Maui, and with my producer. At present I'm in Michigan—I know not where God will take me, but I'm ready for His leading. Although

I was born here and love it—I have experienced *horrendous* culture shock. Everyone is wonderful, but I left so much love and memories behind in California. There is not a day without pain of loss. I know God has His reasons and will give me strength for what lies ahead.

Also in coming to Michigan I left behind my keyboardist—she was lovely and so talented! I began searching, I prayed and went through much agony while waiting for someone to fill this need. I had some leads but after each audition I was back to searching again. Some weeks later, with suggestion from my niece, I had left a message for a college student at Ferris State University, Michigan, to call me. She was stated as a "talented musician."

A few days passed; the phone rang and a sweet voice on the other end introduced herself as Luisa. I stated my reason for asking her to call me, and almost immediately we were bonded. Somewhere out there God had been directing two longing souls to this moment. I told Luisa how I had become discouraged and began to think God did not want me to sing. She then joined in with how she had been praying and searching for God to use her for His Kingdom. We set a time to meet and with thrill in our hearts, we expressed to each other that we knew God had definitely brought us together and said good-bye.

A few days later we got together at Ferris State University, Michigan, for rehearsal. Though the thrill of our connection remained within our hearts, we both sensed the great need for preparatory work. Luisa is a classical pianist—trying to accompany a vocalist does not come all that easily, for classical pianists have their own interpretations.

Two weeks later we meet again. Some improvement was noted, but yet the fact remained we still had further exertion before us. I was certain Luisa would lose heart before this perfection was completed.

Now—Several weeks had passed since our last rehearsal. Luisa had been occupied with college papers and exams. We meet at the church this time. We proceed with our concert format and before long a warm feeling begins to sweep through my entire body. I couldn't believe my ears. I began singing "We Shall Behold Him" and part way through I knew this little earthly angel was very serious about what she set out to do. We made eye contact and I'm sure both of us were holding back tears. I also knew without a doubt that long ago God had our mission all mapped out.

After many rehearsals and continuous praying, we now are ready for stage and our first upcoming concert. We have been invited to Puerto Rico and the Hawaiian Islands as well as churches throughout the United States.

A few evenings ago I called Luisa and asked her to tell me her story behind the following words she so often says to me: "I am so thrilled and honored to be part of your mission." Somehow those words penetrate my soul with sweet depth and honesty. I listen quietly now as Luisa devotedly expresses her story I asked of her. "Last year at December break I attended a Christian Youth Rally. During the rally I became very close to the Lord and felt I was being called for His service. I wanted to do it now—not later. Later might be too late, as I sensed the soon coming of Christ. I began searching, thinking possibly, God wanted me as a missionary in some foreign land. I became weary, nothing seemed to come about but still I remained on fire to my call.

One day I returned home from school and turned on

my messages. There was a message for me to call Ramona. I called, and after a brief conversation, my heart knew this was God's answer to my prayer. It was soon after my birthday and I also knew it was God's birthday gift to me."

I know this story will touch your hearts as it has touched my heart. It is so awesome when the young choose to give their all to the glory of God. Luisa is thrilled and honored because it is God she is serving. Luisa comes to us from the Dominican Republic.

. . . if you seek the Lord your God, you will find Him if you look for Him with all your heart and with all your soul. . . . For the Lord your God is a merciful God. . . . Deuteronomy 4:29 and 31 NIV.

Singing has not always had its joys. Several years ago, surgery was done on my throat; accidentally my vocal chords were damaged. I had to learn to use them all over again. It took hours, days, months—yes, even years. My young son Louis would say: "Mummy your voice sounds funny." Yes—that hurt, but bless his little heart, in his child-like innocence he spoke. Then the day came when he joined in with me as I practiced my opera pieces. He sang them with perfect pitch from memory. Billy, along with his singing, chose the guitar for his musical love. Debbi loved the piano, but spent much time writing poetry. Ramona Lynn enjoyed playing several musical instruments, but excelled on the clarinet.

Today my voice is much softer. Perhaps that is the way God wants it. God can do what He wants. He only needs our willingness.

10
Keep Walking

You have walked with me through some beautiful times, and some not so lovely times—some very painful and hurtful. Together we will search for some meaning that will perhaps help each of you to identify some of your heartaches and also resurrect some hidden beauty, wisdom and talent yet to be explored.

In this nefarious world of organized crime, narcotics, and organ farming secondary to greed, it is somehow becoming a lost cause to reach out—in fact, scary. But God lives, and still is in control, letting us possess the vein of beauty that flows from the cross.

In depth we can gather sprinkles of rain to provoke more growth. Each drop adds its power that forms the mighty oak. Remembering the closer we get to God the more we must battle with the forces that attempt to hold us back. Some of us have seen actual battles of conflict between good and evil, making us wiser to the reality of this world. We are not in a world of flesh and blood but of powers and principalities. God seems abandoned—let us look diligently for His presence.

At this moment of thought, I'm pulled to the great outdoors. I love awakening to the sounds of the sweet mourning dove. Oh, how memories seem to dance before my eyes, bringing laughter but also tears. Out my upstairs window I can gather the reflection of the sun upon the lake giving forth glitter of gems, yet pawing me with cryptic sensation.

Then in the evening when the light of day gently fades into the arms of darkness and the loon and crickets cast their spell of enchantment, I again let my eyes open to old and new impressions. What a beautiful God that moves through people and time to commune with us.

My heart is so very touched just now. I'm moved as I pull knowledge and emotion as though it were a first. As I continue my walk my whole being electrifies as I'm once again shown the beauty, love, and inspiration that spiritual love radiates. Perhaps just now before you read on you can sit back and think upon special spiritual loves.

Together words and music are invented. What a powerful and amazing God to capture people from the world— bring them together in perfect harmony to musically create and to lift the hearts of men with harps and strings of gold. Man's path is graced. Nothing is more beautiful and sensational than God's touch on man.

God loves us so much. He delights as we His children feed from the beauty and love that He so graciously gifted. All of us have spiritual hunger at times—this indeed wakes up the soul!

The flow of my pen reveals God to me in so many ways as it will do for you. Let your body and soul catch these moments that they slip not from you to find another resting place. Life passes so quickly; we see it not until we long to say, to do, to hear again all that we lost. Take a moment to speak a tender word. Drop a rose in the path of a cherished friend. Slip away with a dear one to catch a snowflake at the mountaintop, or to the ocean floor to feel the splashing waves upon the rocks as laughter greets you there a while.

My friend, do not close your ears to wisdom. Let no one tug your soul to lesser place. Let wisdom grow and love with it. Be gentle and careful that all are made strong or weakness and ignorance could be your chant.

Let me share with you now some thoughts that at one time or another plague all of us. It doesn't matter—child, youth, man or woman, from all walks of life we head for the clouds, knowing that one day, one hour, we have to descend. Tuning out until tomorrow does not set us free. And believe me, though we, for all intents and purposes, quote, "have everything stabilized," we do fall prey. So with me, dear ones, let your hearts be sensitive. Go ahead, sob, shed tears, and let tenderness caress the inner soul—it emerges a beauty that is soft as a summer rain. The stranger in us will find a friend.

Each day, though it flows in purpose, gathers from its joys and hopes only to find a stopping place. There we stand face to face with doubt, fearing the morrow—finances, work or home disasters, romance and sudden upheaval. Yes man, behind his rigid membrane, tries to pass over his boundaries to become vulnerable. None desire to lose or be rejected, especially of all we cherish—health, talents, profession, family, friends, things, or one that is most dear to us. Many times we play games with ourselves and each other, changing our personalities. We keep dark, hidden secrets concerning self only to learn true love changeth not but endures all things. We pull apart for seasons to dodge that horrible thing called "exposure." Yes, fear, terrible, terrible fear. So we hold back leaving self and others in agony—agony of the worst kind. What sadness and exhaustion arises out of this sequence of events. A dear friend often spoke of how much he wished he could find all those he hurt to say: "I'm so sorry"—perhaps he will find me one day. . . Faith needs a reintroduction. Faith in God, self and in our fellow man. It is, however, most difficult to accomplish this when life has dealt with us cruelly. At this time we need to go back and take God's hand and walk with Him. It is when we let go of His hand that life presents options that lead to our own destruction. We must step out in boldness and stand firm in faith; then we acquire a strong existence.

Think seriously upon the following reflection: There is nothing quite as wonderful as experiencing trust; a virginal trust we gift to a friend. About friends, loyal of loyals. Oh, how terrifying when put to the test—loss of riches, glamour, beauty, talent, and earthly lovelies. Interludes, frightening to say the least. Can the grasp of hand feel its slow release? After the desert storm and the winds of sand slowly lay to rest, where is the silhouette? Must the flowing white gown be gathered to wipe the tears as one sinks to the ground? Have faith sweet ones, for yet a little while. After the storm the rainbow, and upon the hill of sand cometh forth the silhouette.

There are times when special friends are mingled with the results of our misfortune. To witness their growth during this adventure is something to behold. I had this awesome experience, but yet to comprehend their stability of character and increase of caring and love has left me without inventive words. For those who have such a friend—never let him go. Let him know how he has and does grace your life. We learn to great depths from manifestations such as this. I'm beautifully reminded of Micah 6:8. "Do justly, love mercy, and walk humbly."

I need humbling. I want to be true—to free myself of all hideous apparel. May God teach me His ways and lead me to a plain path. Though I sit upon my stair steps with tears on my cheeks and walk frail through the day, my God has hold of me. I beg of God—don't let go.

Keep Walking

Many times upon my stair steps I see my life and once again review the hurts and pain . . . not of just yesterday but of today. Many things go unknown to those who walk beside me—sometimes to those who caused the pain. Why? Because our life and hurts are swallowed up in silence. I like to remember at these times what a dear friend said after walking through a recent hurt with me: "One more ripple upon the water can't hurt you can it?"

Also on my stair steps I praise God. I praise Him for all His mercies—love—and for all His help. For all the times He caught me when I was falling. I praise His beautiful creation and kingdom and the beauty of His holiness. I'm so thankful for music—music to set me free and to honor His Holy name.

Often on my stairs I think of a special woman who turned my life around—Sister Catherine from St. Joseph's College. She had asked me to sing at the Mother House in Portland, Maine. I did—what a mountaintop experience that was! Sister Catherine wrote: "The night you sang in our Mother House chapel was such a happy memory for me—I re-live it often. You are one of the inspirations of my life—truly a woman who walks with your God and searches for truth." Each time I open the door to her memory and other touching memories I cry softly.

People have given so much, especially when my heart was so crushed. It is so good to take time out for silences—to open these doors. Doors to God, friends, family and thoughts that touch heart strings. This heals, builds character, softens the soul and carries beauty to the beholder. These moments are so precious—precious in ways that tell us how beautiful all the souls that reach out. They give their time and hearts to help when all seems lost . . . they are there. That is awesome!

11

Human Compassion

    I would like to step back in time for a brief moment to other periods of influence upon my life. We think walking through life is unbearable at times. Could it be we miss the final pain of man? After heartbreak and break-up I waltzed through doors of a nursing home—AKA "extended care" today. Somehow my whole being began to speak to me. Had I been so struck in my own anguish that another part of my world knew not of those tucked away from love, work and play as they once had known it? My heart slowly felt a horrible emptiness for all I was about to behold.
    Time and change has taken man from his cherished surroundings and placed him in a forcible restraint to await his final breath of air. Perhaps there is no other way. What a curse to the tender soul. Can we, do we, make efforts to release such agony?
    Most nursing facilities give their best to invite some sunshine into the hearts of heartbroken occupants. We know, however, that at best much is lacking. The ever present turnover of staff takes away the security of residents time and time again. Though employer carefully seeks staff of caring nature, let it be known all can be misled. As a result some residents are abused mentally and physically. Of course there are some folk that accept their condition and are grateful for the good care they

get and do enjoy visiting with other residents. Some, who have lived alone, are better off and more content in extended care.

Then we have the family—sometimes very caring and attentive if we can redirect them beyond their guilt. All do experience guilt when one finally realized the outcome of placing a loved one in a nursing facility. And, there are times when no other way is possible.

Perhaps some of the following knowledge can help us to better understand the dynamics involved with placement of loved ones in confinement. First, what precipitated the decision for placement. Some may have had previous illnesses (mental and physical) that eventually escalated to plateaus of unpredictable stability. No one was able to provide twenty-four hour care and placement was a given. Others may have lost their mates, who helped in their care and the worst scenario for them crashed right in their front yard. They not only have not their loved one, but now they have to leave home—giving up loved one, home and privacy for a place of eternal strangeness. They are sick, helpless and with all taken from them, even their self respect and dignity. I'm sure this pain will never grip us until we become the victim.

Their whole life now is living for a card, a phone call, a visit from a loved one. And after all this comes to pass—than back to aloneness. All the things that once brought joy and peace now come back to haunt.

Personalities change. Why? They cry out for help or for someone to listen—instead they become classified as the grumbler.

The patient would love to go out for a meal, attend his or her church of choice or travel again.

It breaks my heart to write upon these pages the outcome of some of our advanced-in-years citizens. How depressing to watch their fellow mates be confined to wheelchair and restraints or even worse to be the victim. And how tormenting for loved ones to watch as mother or father, sister or brother, wife or husband become more and more confused as diseases of the mind and body speed up their deficiencies. We as staff long for more time to give love and an ear, but days come and go and we are still longing to be what we can't be!

Listening one to one and conversations of residents I find they wish that more children from churches would be sent to sing and talk with them. They love children and animals.

Loved ones long for the pastors of churches to give an occasional call to them or drop by to see how they are coping. They feel this happens all to seldom.

Days seem to fade into another lonely day. Days of hopelessness and helplessness.

As staff and relatives we know all cannot be fixed, but just maybe each of us can take a closer look into our hearts and bring about some longed-for joy that is realistic!

Today, March twenty-fourth, my day of birth! I awakened to a beautiful gift of falling snow. The prairie-like land was dressed with sparkles of white. At seven a.m. I wrapped myself with clothing of warmth and made my way down the country road. It is such a thrill to make first etchings upon the snow. The gentle falling flakes touched my cheeks while the howling wind caught my scarf and whirled it all about. The flying geese seemed to cry out: "We returned home too soon." Each little bird hovered over its nest, telling me—do not disturb. Mother nature is at work here. The quick little squirrel made haste over the snow as he heard my approaching footsteps. I stopped to sing to the huddled cattle: "The Hills are Alive with the Sound of Music." I haven't quite figured out if they like my floating melodies or if they stand in wonderment of such behavior. As for me, it brings tingles—just to watch their devotion and awe! We can learn much from such occurrence. My walk was nearing end when a young deer pranced the field at a distance. One can see God's charm in the grace of a dancing deer. They are so beautiful and exciting.

As I traveled on from extended care I entered the world of acute mental problems, chemical dependency and eating disorders. Talk about heartaches of extended care—I had yet to face the ghastly existence of those who have mental disturbances.

Unless one has walked where they walk or has connected through their daily care there is no way to envision all that torments their souls. I will start with the dear youth—some very young. I can't begin to tell you the tearing at my heart to hear and watch the struggles of their existence. How does one break down the years of imprinting to introduce new thoughts, feelings and emotions, especially when one has been traumatized—physically and mentally.

Many times I was called to a room to listen while a youth poured out his or her fears and hurts. I needed a much stronger heart than I had. Sometimes it took every drop of strength I had to fight back the emotions that turned me inside out. It is true some were very good actors, but unfortunately for the most, it was real. Due to confidentiality I will not expose details. However, one of the greatest fears of all youth is dying. Why? They cannot give their devotion to parents anymore. They must belong to a gang or their life is definitely in danger, and of course it is not safe there either—a catch twenty-two.

Day after day one has to walk away from place of employment with this heavy burden knowing that some of these issues will never get solved. With some, their hurts and pains have been so deeply ingrained that they have fallen into a world of fantasy—hoping to find fulfillment there. All of us build our own kingdoms, and sometimes go to meaningless lengths to protect that kingdom. God and only God can bring us to a better place, but He first needs our consent.

When people become hardened due to life-long trauma, it is so difficult to remain a friend or be a support, but I find myself not wanting to let them go. Why? Because they need someone so badly to care for them and to love them. They may abuse you mentally, and even become sadistic and very calculating. However, if one can rise above their station in life, and understand their existence without permitting them to destroy you, then you perhaps can stand by their side in hopes the barrier will come down one day. It will take all the love you can give, and unequaled stability of anything else you have ever pursued.

Many times we are faced with letting go. The hardest part is knowing that each of us is a child of God. Whatever we do to one another we are doing it to Christ. That thought is just a killer—especially if you love and care deeply for your fellow man. I'm beginning to feel something of how terrible God feels when one of His sheep goes astray. He must weep intensely!

I try so hard to look beyond pain and hurts in others that I might understand their sometimes unbearable behavior. The most difficult is knowing when to give up. That is my greatest fear and agony. I want so much for all to have the chance for progress; especially when it comes to their happiness.

I know each of us at times in our life find ourselves searching, weeping and with agony—perhaps induced by carelessness of a friend, loved one, family or a significant other. One of the worst pains outside of losing a loved one is to be under the influence of inflicted pain from a special person in your life. When disappointments come and break-up becomes inevitable there is only one solution: accept the pain and trust the mourning days to the Lord. It seems as though morning will never be again! I have found that by asking God for peace within, even though the pain is there, at least one can continue on as he heals. It takes tremendous faith to achieve this victory, however God is as strong for us as we ask Him to be. As previously mentioned, our hurts and pains are difficult to quiet.

Sometimes all I can hear is the strength of the waves dashing against my ship and filling my soul with fear. Struggles begin and with anguish and tears I ask my God . . . where are you? Many times from my voyage at sea I come to God. With Him I share the secrets of my heart.

During heartbreak the events that created such pleasure for us now come back to haunt us through our memories. It is as though all the sweetness is insufferable to even think upon—one just wants to close the door to his hall of memories and deny that they are there. He even asks: "Did I really have what I thought I had?" That is even more frightful and painful! For all who love and lose, time will relax the pain, but time never removes the lingering sign of damage. The sun, moon and stars now bring a different glow. I listen to the sounds of God's creation but sometimes I hear only silence. How wonderful it is to look deep enough in the human soul and to bring to light all the beautiful qualities that rest there. We need to love and seek to understand each other. We need to ask for the fruits of the Holy Spirit that our lives will enhance the beauty around us—transform the common into something precious. Oh how sad for man to be alone and with sorrow.

Thank You Lord

Thank you Lord for the trials that come my way
In that way I can grow each day
As I let you lead

And Thank you Lord for the patience those trials bring
In that process of growing
I can learn to care

But it goes against the way I am to put my human nature down
and let the spirit take control
of all I do

'Cause when those trials come, my human nature shouts
the thing to do
and God's soft prompting can easily be ignored

I thank you Lord for each trial I feel inside
that You're there to help lead
and guide me away from wrong

'Cause you promised Lord that with every testing
that Your way of escaping
is easier to bear

But it goes against the way I am to put my human nature down
and let the spirit take control
of all I do

'Cause when those trials come, my human nature shouts
the thing to do
and God's soft prompting can easily be ignored

I thank you Lord for the victory that growing brings,
in surrender of everything
life is so worthwhile

And I thank you Lord when everything's put in place
Lord up front I can see your face—
and it's there you belong. . . .

Dan Burgess

12
I Thank You Lord

I can't help feeling at this moment the wonderment of eyes to see, ears to hear, a voice to express, and a voice to sing—a mind to grasp the abilities to display these endowments and the physical command to perform. As I walk daily to my country mailbox I marvel at such abilities. We should never take all these precious gifts for granted—let it ever be before us just how magnificent our God is.

At this moment I am embraced by a new spring—I carefully watched the tiny buds upon the trees as they slowly matured into delicate green leaves. How awesome! God's creation! I marvel beyond comprehension, and can't let go of this thrill that stirs my soul I am so taken in by all this beauty, yet I am reminded of my dear sister's death just before Spring two seasons ago. I miss her so. We shared so much. Nothing can ever fill the emptiness left in my heart.

I am still passing through heartache. Many heartaches! I asked the Lord to give me grace while passing through. But it wasn't until in desperation I asked: "Lord, what is it you want me to learn just now?" that I found peace. God gave me the answer almost immediately. I felt a warm sensation surge through my whole being. I heard these words: "Do good to those that hate you—love your enemies—be merciful—be good to those that despitefully use you." I since feel a sweet tenderness towards those that are oppressive. It took some time before I asked the above question. I wasn't ready to ask. Now I feel the hurt of the abuser. The inflicter has so much pain that he can't possibly see that he is abusing. We mustn't accept evil behavior towards us, but we can pray for each other and keep a tenderness in our hearts that we can be a blessing instead of a curse. I now have greater peace within. Sometimes I am so touched by the inflicter's pain that my pain is overcome through his pain. We need to remove the Pharaohs from our hearts that we can serve God.

I feel as though I'm on a voyage at sea, broken at times, but praising God for all that He is teaching me. I love the following words of David: "Show me thy ways, O Lord; teach me thy paths. Lead me in thy truth, and teach me: for thou art the God of my salvation; on thee do I wait all the day." As we stand on the seashore of life; how many ships will pass us by?

13
Tender Trap

The following is dedicated to someone dear. Someone that traveled through miles of agony—one that looked only once upon her newborn baby's face; then released her child to another. That moment no one can comprehend nor can one understand events that trigger such a grave misfortune. Dear one, know that God placed within you a little creature to protect and love while He developed him into a magnificent, brilliant, talented and glorious being. No one can understand why such choices are made for us, but God is in control and one day will make all things plain. Each of us has thorns in our life. God is watching over us. More often than not we see not the reasons nor do we understand the "WHYS," but we do have the promise: "Lo, I am with you always."

Moments ago, a little bird hit my window. Oh, how that grips at my heart! Tears flow immediately. I want to do something, but I am so helpless! I love my large bay windows, but resent the fact that my joy is a danger to the birds. Sometimes the birds fall dead quickly, other times they rest on the ground until they come to their senses. Today, this beautiful little bird let me place him or her in my hand, but not without profuse chirping. I actually pet the bird. About one half hour later the bird flew away. That is one of my greatest joys to see the recovery of a little bird after a crash! And to think: God knows every bird that falls. How glorious and magnificent, our God! How blessed we are to be part of His kingdom. God is so near—the skies with streaks of gold and snow with sparkles of diamonds ever tell us: <u>He is near!</u>

Yes, our God is so Majestic! Recently I happened upon a most beautiful sunset—unique! I have experienced within the last two years such unusual phenomena in the skies—wondering at those times if others saw what I saw. I wish so much I could describe the whole. But I realize that is impossible! Regardless of how good or bad a day we are having, enchantment is ours everyday. To try to explain the enchantments would alter its glory! Among these valued moments I watched as the day claimed the stars, and the big dipper was upside down. Never had I observed such miracles. I was walking down my country road at the time, and two little stars guided me to my door. Shortly thereafter the heavens were twinkling with millions of stars! I share these intervals of time with you, for they heal when life is so heavy. They also bring wisdom to our being. Take time to search the skies for paintings from God. They are there, and created just for you.

The following I wish to share with you, for each of us is individualized and has idiosyncrasies. People don't always tolerate who we are. It is wonderful when we meet folk, and yes, even loved ones that accept us just the "way we are." Not too long ago I received a page at work—"You are wanted on line one." I picked up the phone and listened while a kind voice said: "I don't think you remember me, but I saw you standing in the hallway today and I'm just certain you had to be the young girl that helped save my life years ago." Of course, I was stirred: "Who could this be?" I invited her to my office, but had little time to talk as I was due for a scheduled conference. It wasn't long before I received a letter from her at my work place: "Every once in a while life hands you a delightful surprise—like a person popping out of the almost forgotten past. Your life touching mine was very brief, but so intense was the experience it was imprinted on my memory for all times. I can still see very vividly that dark corner room in the basement of the old hospital, the light flashing on, and you and your mother walking in like ministering angels—and you truly were. You and your mom inspired such confidence. The other day when I saw you standing outside your doorway at work I felt mistaken in calling you, but as we talked I could again see the girl you were—in your eyes and the shape of your face. What pain you must have gone through when you lost your young son. And what strength you must have, to have turned that grief into a positive outpouring of music from your soul." When discouraged and tempted to turn away from my music ministry, I try to renew the image of words such as the above, to help me continue in the path God has sketched for me.

14

Take My Hand

In heartache and trial, we sometimes feel as a stranger in the land, like a fawn coming to the field for the first time. Sometimes we laugh when we should cry, and even dare to paint a new sky. God wants so much for us to develop a trust that will carry us through times of all doubt. I know, even now, as I write upon this page I keep asking God for that trust. I believe there is a God, therefore I should have complete trust in Him. Though my pain is unbearable, I want to say in my heart: "You love me Lord—you want joy for me, your child—I trust you with my life!" Dear friends, don't weaken, it does take time and energy to leave all at the feet of Jesus. He loves us so much. We have to keep focus on that matchless love that we can rest assured that He sees the end from the beginning, and will not take <u>anything</u> from us that is for our joy or good. Lean on His everlasting arms! I want so much to pick up the cross and follow Jesus. I know to do that, God has to clear my path.

Trust God with those we have loved so much who vanish unexpectedly in our life. What a test! But God is refining our house! Some heartaches we must trust completely to God, for many we never understand. I feel so safe in the arms of Jesus. I have so much evidence of His love, and better insight to His purpose. "Many are the plans in a man's

heart, but it is the Lord's purpose that prevails!" The following I wrote one evening while under deep duress:
"Lord in the morning, let me hear—your voice so tender, loud and clear. . . .
May it take me through the day—until the night comes home to play.
There I'll stay within your arms—until the morn bring back her charms. . . ."

For those who love music—go to it! It uplifts and brings God near and fills our souls with ecstasy. And those who have musical talents—use them for the Lord. They will reach the rich and poor, the lowly and proud, and the strong and weak. I love many types of music—my most favorite is Rachmaninov Concerto No. 2 in C minor, Op 18. Each time I hear it performed I wonder how heaven can produce still greater sensation!

The days grow dim now, for all bathe in sorrow beyond understanding, but it is my prayer that all who pain will open your hearts to the love and presence of your Heavenly King. Our Majestic King! I cannot direct enough attention to His love and caring for all. He <u>longs</u> for us to call upon Him—in joy and pain. We are forever inscribed in His heart.

As I approach the end of my writings I want all to know, that in spite of adversities in my life, God has blessed me beyond all imagination. "Somewhere in my youth or childhood, I must have done something good."

The world will continue to manifest its wretchedness . . . we need to turn our eyes upon Jesus. "You will show me the path of life; In your presence is fullness of joy; At your right hand are pleasures forevermore." What awesome words! They are powerful, beautiful, profound and should be written upon our hearts for daily delectation. May God help us all as we stand for Him! Don't go inward—go to God! Let sadness find its place in the desert. Serve man, for then we serve God! How awesome, one day we will witness as man bows down to our Majestic King in the earth made new!

My brother Ned devoted his life to humanity. There were times his heart was torn as he stood between man and maybe twenty years of his life in confinement. "Grown men cry or place an arm about you. I never fail to realize that in Polygraph during the examination there is the subject being examined and the examiner in the room. There is a third person that you cannot see; but believe me He is constantly there. In fact, at times you can almost feel Him in the room. Because, let's face it, here again in dealing with the human element, you can get, or rather experience, the most lonely feeling in the world!"

Our God shall reign forever and ever—King of Kings and Lord of Lords!

May all have courage to go forward in Christ, no matter the cost. God be with everyone.

The power and magic of winter has ended. The white rose now sends forth her beauty!
When all seems lost and tears begin to flow beyond control ... call ye upon your God. You will feel the presence of angels! Sit upon the rock by the brook and let its music bring forth the sweet memories of life. God guards our hearts and stills the storm. One day soon we will walk in the beautiful land that God is preparing for us. Remember the trials shared with you upon these pages. ... They will help you to know—We can, be happy in our sorrow. ...

Take my hand. ... Walk with me!